TOWARD A MATURE FAITH

by
ERWIN R. GOODENOUGH

PRENTICE-HALL, INC.
NEW YORK

Copyright 1955 by
PRENTICE-HALL, INC.

COPYRIGHT UNDER
INTERNATIONAL AND PAN-AMERICAN
COPYRIGHT CONVENTIONS

All rights reserved, including the right to reproduce this book, or portions thereof, in any form, except for the inclusion of brief quotations in a review.

LIBRARY OF CONGRESS CATALOG CARD NUMBER: 55-6264
PRINTED IN THE UNITED STATES OF AMERICA

For Evelyn

CONTENTS

1. PERSONAL 1
2. DEPTH PSYCHOLOGY:
   WISH PROJECTION 33
3. DEPTH PSYCHOLOGY: SYMBOLS 51
4. FAITH 70
5. HOPE 94
6. LOVE 110
7. SALVATION 137
8. JESUS IN THE NEW AGE 158
9. PERSONAL AGAIN 176

Toward a Mature Faith

1

PERSONAL

This little book is a report on a long spiritual search. The solution to which I have come after many years is one which, like all spiritual solutions, will seem quite unacceptable to some people. Yet it is a thoroughly realistic solution, one which I know many people are looking for. And it is a solution in which spiritual values still seem to be the most important element in human life. I am not a philosopher in the sense that I have a systematic body of ideas about the nature of man and the universe. Still less am I a theologian who professes he can expound the nature of God. Actually I am a very pragmatic fellow, indeed so pragmatic that I want to use everything which seems to have value.

Among the things that I as an individual have found valuable, and I as a historian see that our ancestors found valuable, are the dreams, the poetic fancies, the symbols of all kinds, which have gone into making up what men have called religion. But what are the values of these things? That has been what all my life I have been trying to find out. And have these things any place in the mid-twentieth century? To me they unquestionably have the most important place of anything in human life.

The best way to come to understand these questions as I am asking them, and the answers to which I have come, will be through the story of my own search. I do not at all intend to write an autobiography in the ordinary sense. My experiences and relations with other people through the years I have no desire to outline. But I have lived a very interesting life within myself, and that life seems to me to be one that may prove suggestive for others.

For now, at sixty, I can see myself as one who has been a part of several civilizations. People younger than I, whose memories begin with the depressed nineteen-thirties or the maniac twenties, have little understanding of the adjustments we, who were coming into maturity when the First World War shattered the civilization which had set our thought-ways, have had to make. And I myself was not only born in the nineteenth century and educated in the Victorian and Edwardian eras, I was brought up in a family which rigidly practiced the Puritanism of the seventeenth century, and cultivated the ecstasies of what in the eighteenth century was sneeringly called "Methodist enthusiasm." Intellectually we belonged to the Romantics of the time of Shelley, though he was too much for us as a group, and we preferred Dickens, Longfellow, and Hannah More. In music we knew only the Romantics, and actually heard them only in sentimentalized renderings. Art and the artificial were quite indistinguishable to us. I shudder to think of the first pictures I bought, to say nothing of those which my parents had on their walls.

To go from such a beginning to the successive decades of the twentieth century—the tens, twenties, thirties, and forties, and now to the problems and thought-ways of the fifties—has taken a good deal of adjustment. A man could always cut himself off, lose himself in a yacht, the country club, or even scholarship. But I moved into the new with a sense of loyalty to what had been of value to me in the past.

Many of these values came from my parents. While I have said that I would not write about my experiences with other people, I must, of course, begin with my parents, for much of our characters and problems originate in our parents, not ourselves.

My father was a fitting product of his Puritan ancestors. He was the seventh child in a family of thirteen children, twelve of whom grew to maturity. The older children were, of course, put out to work to help feed this colony as soon as they could hold a hoe, and so they got little education. My father was the first exception. He was allowed to work his way through the Academy five miles away, and through Hamilton College, after which he read law in the office of a lawyer in

Ogdensburg, was admitted to the bar, and went to New York to seek his fortune. From his mother, indeed from all of his ancestry except his own father, he got the great Puritan heritage of adjustment to life by hard work. One of my uncles once described Grandpa Goodenough to me by using a four-letter word so obscene that he had to drop his voice to say it: "Your grandpa was *lazy!*" Certainly my father was not lazy. Once in a blue moon he would play checkers with us, but normally he worked from early morning till late at night. He could do anything from carpentry of the most beautiful finish to making my mother a dress. But men who took vacations, who played golf or tennis, were to him sinful wastrels. Tobacco, alcohol, profanity, and any hint of salaciousness were anathema to him.

His severity I have never seen equalled. A rebuke from him was a thrashing in itself. Actually he rarely rebuked us—he had only to look his displeasure. At the table when we three children began to get out of hand he had only to tap his ring on his plate to stop instantly all quarrelling. Any yapping dog would cringe, and crawl under a table, at a word from him. He was superintendent of a large Sunday school for many years, and never raised his voice to speak to the gathering. When he called the three hundred children to order he simply rang a small bell once, and then stood and looked at them. He rarely had to wait more than twenty seconds for the hall to become electrically hushed.

All of this was the result of his severity with himself. A man so passionate that every pretty woman inflamed him, he not only checked any inkling of flirtation; he "buffeted himself" until all thought of desire had vanished. His favorite aphorism was, "We cannot keep the birds from flying over our head, but we can keep them from making nests in our hair." His favorite verse was, "As a man thinketh in his heart, so is he." A man filled with bitterness and repressed aggression to the point that the only humor he knew was that which arose from a situation in which someone was thwarted or humiliated, he never to my knowledge did a retaliatory act to anyone who injured him, or spoke resentfully of him. On the contrary, his life was a succession of unknown deeds of kindness. In later life, in the years when he had some money, he put boy after boy through college, gave them the money with the one requirement that they never tell a soul where it came from or he would not give another cent. As I watched the procession before my father's coffin my mother said to me, "That's a boy he put through college." "That's a boy he made able to become a beautiful organist." On and on they passed. I had not known a fraction of it. And we all sang his favorite hymn, "Work! for the night is coming, when man works no more."

How much this character of my father was a product of his religion, and how much his religion was a product of his character, I shall never know. The two were completely a unit as I grew up with him. "God and my father" was not a subject for comedy in our family. No believer in hell fire, and so far as I could see

Toward a Mature Faith

with no trace of that terror to drive him into religion, my father lived under a God who in every sense of the term was strictly good. Christ was his elder brother, kindly, loving, who demanded my father's all in return for that love. My father gave Christ his all. Not a mystic in the sense I shall describe in my Uncle Charlie, my father walked and talked with Christ, for, in his favorite phrase, he had "given himself to Christ." To me as a boy his taciturnity, his unrelaxing work, his severity, made him an unapproachable, unknown superman, the sort of father indeed from which gods are made. From him I learned many values—more than I shall ever myself understand. But we never met, even after I had grown up. We sat by his bed as he was dying in the agony of a thrombosis. One of his few remarks was to look over at us and say, "You folks are having a high old time, aren't you?" His only consolation through those hours was frequently to sip water with a lot of quinine powder dissolved in it. He liked the bitter taste.

With such a father, a little boy would naturally turn for warmth to his mother, and here warmth was never lacking. When my mother was quite old, my sister, a psychiatrist, gave her an intelligence test, and found that she was really high. We could hardly believe it, for she herself had been the leader in developing the family tradition that she was not clever like Papa, but quite stupid. She too was a northern New Yorker of old Puritan stock. My father fell in love with her when he had just finished college, and a more devoted wife never lived. "I have never questioned his judgment on anything," she told me many times; and it was true. Her opinions in business and of people were often sounder than his, but she never insisted on them, and never lost the sense of his infallibility even after his decisions, against her advice, led him to financial ruin. Her very devotion ultimately cloyed on him, and the old relation clearly disappeared, so far as he was concerned, for their last twenty years together. But she never admitted it to herself for a second, or changed her blind loyalty. When he died she passionately wanted to die also so that she could be with him in heaven, for heaven to her was to be with him, even more vividly than with God or Jesus.

She was as warm with us children as my father was cold. She had been a very pretty girl, of the hearty peasant type, but soon after she was married she developed a great goiter which disfigured her for twenty-five years before she had it removed. It made her socially very shy, and aggravated the sense of inferiority she had been forcing upon herself from girlhood. But she had a wonderful instinct for a humorous situation, and would come home and re-enact it in a way to make us explode in gales of laughter—all of us but my father, whose disapproval finally made her give up such levity. She gave up so much of herself in that way that she was really quite insipid in her later years. But her earlier vivacity, her sense of humor, registered deeply in my early years, and became one of my best heritages. She used to read Dickens to us, while we all together bellowed in one way at his humor, and in another at his pathos, each equally loudly. Her warmth went outside to anyone in trouble. A stream of girls and women came to her for comfort all the while.

The comfort she had to give was partly her own warm sympathy and really good understanding, but also the assurance that all troubles disappeared in the peace given by God. This was by no means a pose with her. Her vivid faith in God's goodness and care for her made it possible for her to pray "Thy will be done" with the complete assurance that she was in the hands of One who would "work all things together for her good," whether those things were joyful or apparently catastrophic. This lesson she taught me thoroughly, so that still today my deepest comfort in trouble is to pray, "Thy will be done."

What did life mean to a sensitive, sickly boy brought up by such parents? First it meant living vividly with God and Jesus as intimate if unseen members of the family. God took on the severity of my father, and Jesus the feminine warmth of my mother. That Jesus was represented to me as a man with a beard helped greatly to relieve my sense of starvation for tenderness and sympathy from my father. But the beard, and the fact that we called Jesus "He," were the only masculine attributes in his character. He had long hair, wore long clothes, and in the pictures of him I know best, the ones by Hoffmann (or by Hoffmann's imitators for Sunday school cards and leaflets), Hoffmann's model had been his wife. Of course I had no idea of all this at the time. But now when I recall my emotions as I sang "Jesus, lover of my soul" I see that the love I envisaged was an enlargement of what I had experienced with my mother. The fact became very important to me later as I tried to understand the place of the Mother Goddess in the lives of devotees of various religions. If my mother could not go with me to school or be present in my difficult relations with the other boys, with whom I could never keep up physically, and who accordingly regarded me as a sissy, Jesus was always there, a constant and vivid presence. Actually, I was indeed a sissy, not that I was feminine but that emotionally I matured very slowly, and until a late age met their cruelty with tears, which of course at once provoked from them greater disgust and cruelty. Jesus probably made me more of a sissy than ever, for though I had passionate resentment toward the other boys for what they did to me, he (and my mother) kept telling me that it would be a sin to fight back, that I must forgive my enemies. That was hardly the path to adjustment in a New York City public school, nor would it be with any group of boys. If repressed resentment, tears, and an illusion of forgiveness were my releases, my compensation was in my mother, and in religion.

The religion of the old Methodist church had two distinct and often quite inconsistent elements. The first was its Calvinistic ethic, which was a legalism as strict as orthodox Judaism, and as segregating. I have often had amusing conversations with Jews, comparing our strictures with theirs. On Sunday we normally went to four services in the church (sometimes five). We read only devotional literature between these services (I never studied a school assignment on Sunday until I was in the twenties), never had a Sunday paper, played only "sacred music" on the piano (the sonatas of Beethoven and Mozart were too worldly). My father did not even allow us to take walks for pleasure, since worldly people did so, and if we were seen on pleasure excursions we might be mistaken for such ourselves. Cards, the theater, and dancing, even in what other people would call their most innocent form, seemed debauchery to us. We had always to bear in mind that we should set an example of godly conduct to our worldly neighbors. We must take no diversion, the motto was, which we could not take in the name of the Lord.

That is, we thoroughly deserved our reputation of being self-righteous prigs, a reputation, and a way of life, which did not at all help my relation with other boys. I look back upon this legalism with incredulity. It was precisely the kind of life which Jesus had denounced in the Pharisees, and yet we cultivated it for Jesus. Still, for all its disadvantages, I know that I learned much good from it which I did not lose when I finally turned against it. It was a magnificent schooling in individualism, in living life as one judged it should be lived regardless of the opinions, or disapproval, of others. Santayana wrote *The Last Puritan* only to show the destructive side of such an attitude. The destructive side was there, certainly, but also a constructive disciplining which created the Yankee individualism that Santayana never came to understand. Goaded by private criteria of value, I have never been able to ride a bandwagon, or keep within any borders set by others. That I am a member of six departments at Yale speaks not for any unique breadth in my learning, but for the fact that conventional boundaries have never meant anything to me. I by no means regret the unhappiness and isolation of my childhood and youth, which my emotional retardation and our strange way of living brought me. I would not revive it for myself or for my children, but I owe to it much that I consider best in me.

This legal discipline threw us also into my father's pattern of work, which I have modified (I never had the physical energy to work the hours he did), but still admire. The greatest pleasure of life is in constructive work. We children picked this up as naturally as we did our parents' way of speaking. I do not recall ever being asked if I had done my homework. When we were twelve, perhaps earlier, my father had to make a strict rule that we should never get up before four o'clock in the morning. Actually, we were not very often up before five. But at that hour we did our lessons and practiced on the piano, and by the time we went to school we had everything behind us, and a free day ahead. All through my life my inner compulsion to work has been also a sense of joy in the creativity of work. It is one of the richest heritages we can give our children.

The other side of old Methodism was equally disapproved by outsiders, its love of free emotional expression of one's love of God and Christ. The Presbyterians, Episcopalians, and members of the Dutch Reformed church—the three socially reputable groups in our community—used to consider us savages. Their sons hung in the windows and jeered as we sang, "Inch by inch we inch along, Inch by inch to Jesus." When I went to their churches, and heard the scarcely audible way in which they sang their more conventional hymns I wondered why they bothered to do it at all. We threw our heads back and sang, we pulsed with the rhythms, and we were thrilled when the minister or one of the older brothers clapped his hands and shouted, "Praise the Lord," or "Glory," because he was so deeply moved. Our songs were mostly passionate love songs: "Nearer my God to Thee," "Draw me nearer, nearer, nearer, Precious Lord," "More love to Thee, O Christ," "I've wandered far away from God, Now I'm coming home," "Blessed assurance, Jesus is mine, Oh what a foretaste of glory divine," "Safe in the arms of Jesus, safe on His gentle breast," "Oh, how He loves," "Jesus loves even me," "Rock of Ages cleft for me, let me hide myself in Thee." We would have been indignantly shocked had anyone pointed out to us the only slightly veiled eroticism in which we were indulging.

But these experiences made me later quite ready to understand the wide place of the libido in human satisfactions, and the appeal which reproductive symbols and cult acts have in civilizations with fewer repressions. The common presupposition of most historians of religion as I read them later is that true reli-

Personal

gion is possible only with the complete exclusion of any sexual motivation and that only as all such elements are excluded can anything worthy to be called true religion emerge. Such an attitude seems to me the product of repression and prudery, though, as we shall see, the whole matter is a highly complicated one. Certainly we Methodists experienced and enjoyed the love of God and Christ. In what seemed to others the crude excesses of our meetings we talked of it, described the ecstasies we had experienced when "Jesus came into our hearts," and as he came to us afresh our faces glowed with joy. In our "testimonies" in the prayer meetings we talked of intimate personal problems and experiences. I remember an old scrub-woman and her husband John, who had never given up his self-will and been converted, though he came with his wife to all the meetings. She stood up and said publicly at our prayer meeting: "Before I found Jesus, my John was everything to me; but since I have found Jesus, my John is nothing to me." I am glad to record that before he died John repented his rebellious spirit and was saved.

I have since come to understand that what other religions, or other branches of Christianity, were doing through symbol and ritual, we were doing directly in immediate expression. We would have been as shocked as any Jew or Catholic if someone had proposed setting up a pagan symbol before the congregation, or in our case, even a holy female image. But we let ourselves go as Catholic saints have often done, and if we had no physical stigmata, we had spiritual and psychological stigmata almost as recognizable. "My beloved is mine, and I am his," the key verse of the Song of Songs, was the keynote of our lives, as it has been of Jewish and Catholic mystics for thousands of years. Those men were wise, I have since come to see, who felt such immediate ecstasies to be dangerous for popular presentation, and who veiled them in symbol and ritual. But I have never lost the impression that to talk about the love of God is a poor substitute for experiencing it.

This was all one facet of the popular world of the nineteenth century. As we saw the world, it was a place of order and, as a whole, basically good. We were only too well aware of the existence of sin about us, and in us. But it was a world where the problems which concerned us were, as we would now see them, relatively trivial. Such problems as drinking, political graft, corrupt business methods, simply represented the need of a good cleaning in a house which had been built by the best of architects, one who always interfered directly when there was any serious emergency. All problems dissolved for us personally, and could be trusted to disappear socially, as the plan of God worked itself out.

I vividly recall my mother's face when she heard of Sarajevo and the possibility of a European war. She registered only bewildered incredulity. That the humanity which God had so well in hand could break out into such sin, she no more could believe than if someone had come to tell her that my father had been caught in the act of rape. Actually it was a number of years before it became apparent to us that the house in

PERSONAL

which we thought we had been living had never really existed. The older generation did not ever recognize the collapse of this dream world, and oddly there are still a great number of people who look back upon it as the golden age to which we must by all means return.

It was basically a world of illusion, and I have no nostalgia for it. In any case it is gone forever. But all my life I have been haunted, and guided, by its dreams. There are always elements of truth in anything by which men have lived with even partial success. At the expense of logical consistency I have clung to those elements from my boyhood while I have gone into a different world, or a series of different worlds. But I am getting ahead of my story.

The greatest new influence in my teens was my Uncle Charlie. He lived in northern New York, and I had met him only rarely when I was smaller, but when I was fifteen the family began going up summers to the tiny village of Pierrepont Manor and using the old Goodenough house which was then his property. Uncle Charlie was a retiring little fellow, the oldest of thirteen children. He was a man of great ability who had had to work from the time when he was a small boy to help support the tribe. Without formal education and caught within the limitations of a rural community, he had risen as high as he could when he became the supervisor of a large dairy farm owned by the one rich man in the community. Limitations! Most readers of this book do not know how for generations in America rural conditions and family obligations have caught some of our best people on the eastern farms, and held them prisoners for life.

Uncle Charlie came to visit me years later when I was a young assistant professor at Yale. He wanted to see everything—the laboratories, libraries, classrooms—and then we sat in my own book-lined study. He was quiet for a moment but suddenly exclaimed, "Erwin, there's no *limit* to it!" He had seen at once that in contrast to his own experience, I was started on an open road, and that nothing would stop me on it but my own lack of resources. If I did not go on to infinity it would be because I myself was finite, not my environment.

The only access Uncle Charlie had to infinity was in religion, and to him religion was just that. He was over seventy before he met a woman he wanted to marry, a nurse who tended him after an operation, but she declined his proposal of marriage. So all his life he turned his intense sexuality likewise into his religious experience, as many of the greatest mystics have done. Aside from punctiliously doing his work, then, religion was indeed the one outlet he had. He became what most people would call a fanatic, but he was a man of extraordinary dynamism. He was steeped in the classics of mysticism—Law, Tauler, Madame Guyon, and the rest—and God gave him all the ecstatic experiences they described.

The devil tried to thwart him in most ingenious ways. Uncle Charlie told me how on one occasion in

Personal

the winter he was wrestling with God for a blessing, and it was just coming through when he heard sleigh bells on the road outside. Automatically, like all good country people of seventy years ago, he rushed to the window to see who was passing, but no one was there, and he returned to his prayer a long way from getting the blessing. He began wrestling again, and again as he reached the height the sleigh bells sounded and he rushed to the window. This time when he saw the empty road he knew it was the devil. He returned to the prayer, and when the bells sounded the third time he kept on praying, and got his blessing.

He had been baptized by the Holy Ghost, for once the roof of the little meeting house had opened to let through a great flame of fire: the flame sharpened down to a cone whose point touched him on the top of his head. It gave him the joy of the Lord, which expressed itself in the "holy laugh." He said people could hear him laughing a mile away, but this I never verified.

The great point which differentiated him from my parents was his ecstatic experiences, and his division of all Christians into those who had been merely "saved" or "converted," and those who had gone on to be "sanctified." Like mystics from Philo of Alexandria onwards, he found this contrast presented in allegory, especially in the migration of the Israelites from Egypt to the Promised Land. The Israelites had indeed left Egypt, the world of sin, and had committed themselves to God by following his leadership in the desert. But

Toward a Mature Faith

theirs had been a sorry experience during those years, nothing but a succession of rebellions and lapses, mitigated by repentance and reinstatement. It was by no means the sort of life which God wanted for them. This was the condition of the great mass of Christians. By the grace of Christ they would go to heaven when they died. But a fuller experience was possible which left such half measures all behind, another state altogether, but it could be attained only by a "death" of all self-assertion. Philo said that the light of God shines into the soul only after all human light has been extinguished. I never heard Uncle Charlie quote this, but it expresses his thought exactly.

This death was a harrowing ordeal. It required giving up every symbol which represented or enhanced the personality. Women had to give up any adornment worn simply as adornment. Uncle Charlie told of one farmer who had difficulty. The blessing simply would not come. My uncle said he looked the man over, and noticed that he was wearing a gold watch and chain. It was the one thing of value in the impoverished family. So he was told that he would not get the blessing until he put these tokens of self-assertion into a drawer and never wore them again. The farmer took this advice only after the most terrific battle with himself, but when the gold was in the drawer he got the blessing. Uncle Charlie knew nothing of psychology in the academic sense, but he was brilliant in spotting the precise impediment, the symbol of self, which, if given up, would mean the total death of self-assertion. Only

PERSONAL

then could a man come to say, "For me to live is Christ," or "Not I live, but Christ liveth in me."

Neither my father nor my mother was ever sanctified, but my elder sister and I were. I see now that the "death" of "self" is only its deep repression in the unconscious, and that such repression is highly dangerous. The self-instincts, what Freud called the "id," try to express themselves in other and unrecognized and hence uncontrolled ways. Especially they tend to appear as spiritual pride, a sense of superiority over those who have not had the experience. While scrutinizing oneself constantly, morbidly, one becomes oblivious of outlets less healthy than bursts of temper or lecherous fancies and acts. Such a cutting in half of oneself is a direct approach to schizophrenia, and many who have tried it have pushed a latent tendency to the point that they have ended in asylums, fully and finally identified in their minds with God or Christ. Fortunately I was not a schizoid by nature, but for a long time I was even further estranged from "reality" than had been the case before. Actually in my case I think it did me great good. I was already a misfit with my schoolmates, one who badly needed self-respect, and if this made me even more remote from them, it gave me a sense of security in my segregation which I could get in no other way. I was a poor student in those years, and my high-school record was very ordinary. During this period I lived entirely in God and in music, playing on the piano and organ frequently five hours a day.

The high point of those years came when I attended a camp meeting with Uncle Charlie, where they were preaching sanctification. When the invitation came for those who wanted the experience I spotted an old farmer and invited him to come up with me to the altar to see if we could pray him through. We succeeded so well that not only was the farmer sanctified, but I was completely overcome, lost all power of walking, and had to be helped out by two men. However far I have come in later years from seeking such rapture, I have never forgotten its reality, and ever since, as I have read the descriptions of ecstatic religious experiences, such as those cultivated by the Dionysiacs, or by the old rabbis in the Temple at the Feast of the Tabernacles, I have felt a sympathy with them which scholarly historians of religion rarely manifest. These experiences are not aberrations, but the logical end of prayer and of most symbolism. Like all logical ends, as the Greeks would have said, it was hazardous in its effects. But I am sure that we understand the middle only as we really know the extremes. Far as I was from having an intellectual approach to or understanding of what I was doing those years, actually the experiences taught me priceless lessons in the depths of the human spirit.

Chiefly I learned from Uncle Charlie what I now would call the surrendering of my id to my ego ideal. For, as I will presently develop more fully, we seem to me to have two warring centers within us. One center, corresponding to Freud's "id," drives us to gratify our physical desires, and to assert our individual superiority over against other people by aggression and cruelty. The other center, which Freud called the "superego" or the "ego ideal," compels us to conform to the standards of society, ethics, and God so that we can be accepted by our environment as proper.

Uncle Charlie taught me to subordinate the first of these to the second. As a result, the other world, the world of spiritual reality, which had already been very vivid to me, now became so real that all else tended to be illusion. Actually, as one emotionally sensitive to his environment, in many ways what Jung likes to call an extrovert, the new attitude created in me as many problems as it settled. But when I later went on into Platonism, and met the distinction that in the physical and social world one has only opinions, more or less right, but that in the ideal world one has true knowledge through a vision given the "eye of the mind," I was in a completely congenial environment. Most scholars in the history of religion that I have known or read have lacked this immediate sympathy with what seems to me an attitude or a craving found in the humblest as well as in the most advanced religions, a craving to "see" and "be seen," a desire to appropriate the divine to oneself as well as to be appropriated into the divine.

Without this general attitude the almost universal change of fertility religions into what the Greeks called mystery religions, for example, is incomprehensible. Uncle Charlie and I both had learned to live vividly, feeling that we were part of a larger reality, in terms of which alone the individual can find meaning. This was by no means an intellectual matter. Our metaphysics were in primeval chaos. But, more importantly, he taught me to "see," and to live in complete appropriation.

This was the boy who went to a small college in which for four years he was still a complete misfit. We studied languages, mathematics, and literature almost exclusively, and my associates in the class and the fraternity found their escape in card playing, bull sessions with no depth or information to guide them, and the extra-curricular activities of athletics, managership, and editorial work conducted in a spirit of rah-rah which I have never seen equalled elsewhere. We were required as Freshmen to sit on the bleachers throughout the fall to cheer the football team as they practiced every afternoon! We were paddled until we were black and blue for the delight of our elders at initiations (I was made black and blue three times), and to teach us to conform to their superior sense of values in life. Our class entered sixty-five members, and graduated thirty-five. The work, that is, was exacting, but there was practically no stimulus for intellectual or social ranging.

I spent four years in a frantic but utterly futile effort to seem to be one of the boys, for I was still basically far behind them in emotional maturity. I lived my life still in religion, in music, and in literature. Contact with the faculty was negligible, for anyone who appeared friendly with a professor was at once dubbed an apple polisher ("super" we called him), and so we were seen speaking with the faculty as little as possible.

Since at the college, either among the boys or faculty, there was no reality with which I could identify myself, I could really live only in dream worlds. And going into those worlds as an escape, I went into them in quite the wrong way. I was the complete sentimentalist in all of them. Literature I read for its thrills, and I read a great deal, but a really critical approach to writing I never was taught or discovered for myself. In music I never developed a basic technique for the organ or piano, though I was college organist for three years. A structural approach to the theory of music I did not know existed. I spent many hours improvising, but it was emotional gush, not music. In my studies my basic competition with my father made Phi Beta Kappa a necessity, but in only one thing did I really take fire. We had to write papers in a course on Shakespeare, and I did two or three on the sources of various plays. Quite unknown to myself I had found my métier. To explain the phenomena of life in terms of its basic sources has been my constant interest. At that time I was ready to attack it in the relatively harmless field of literature. My professor encouraged me with the idea that I had started a promising doctor's dissertation, so I planned to go on in that field when I left college.

In religion there was little advance. I was slightly secularized by life in the fraternity house, to the point, for example, that Sophomore year I began to dance;

but smoking, drinking, profanity, and obscenity were still unthinkable. While many of the boys were interested in the Y.M.C.A., I was again a misfit in that group. Their much more mature and realistic adjustment to the life of the college was beyond me. Still I lived my life almost alone with the evangelical Jesus.

In the summer between Junior and Senior years, the dread summer of 1914, I had a remarkable new religious experience in which I went through the gamut of agonies of guilt at certain peccadillos. In the course of these agonies I felt that if God reinstated me I should go into the ministry, and this was the solution of the crisis. I returned to college more remote from the group than ever. My roommate, a raw Freshman from an upstate village, I converted to Jesus in my sense of the term, but I left college at the end of the year with great relief, planning to go into the ministry and to take a Ph.D. in English. What this meant, I now see, was that the ministry was the emotional expression of my life, while my intellectual drive was to be kept in the dream world of literary history. That the two drives, the drive to emotional experience and the drive to creative understanding, could have any relationship to each other, be coordinated into a single drive, had not yet entered my head.

After a summer in English at Columbia I attended two Methodist seminaries each for a year, and since my Greek and Hebrew were both well advanced at entrance, I finished in two years. During the next two summers and for week ends through the year between,

Personal

I had a little parish in a village on the great corn plain of Illinois, and discovered that I was a very effective preacher. At the same time I responded with deep enthusiasm to the courses where we did any historical analysis of Christian history and doctrine. In the second year I awoke to the fact that I was a most promising young preacher who both philosophically and historically had no idea what he was talking about. It was not for many years that I discovered that I was just as naïve psychologically. I was like an excellent driver without the slightest idea of where his car had come from, or what made it go, though as a minister I was setting up as a spiritual repair man.

The interest in the analysis of Shakespeare's sources now shifted to a genuinely realistic problem, the problem of the origin and nature of religion. I had had enough work in theology proper to feel quite estranged from its approach. For me to go on in theology or philosophy seemed silly; at best I could hope only to work out one more metaphysical system. Suddenly there was born an aspect of my life, which had never appeared before because of my escapism into spiritual or literary or musical worlds. Without at all putting it to myself in this form, I had discovered that I was essentially an empiricist who thought in terms of documents and evidence, not in terms of logical relevancies. As I expressed it then, what I needed was a little more information. Perhaps at the remote age of forty, or even sixty, I would have a philosophical position. Now I needed a few facts about where Christianity had come from, how it became what it did and so what were its deepest and permanent values. It was at last a search for values in the real world in terms of their origins. I by no means gave up the sense of reality of my spiritual experiences. Jesus was still vividly with me. As I went to Harvard and had a little parish in Holbrook, Mass., I preached to my simple congregation more movingly than ever.

Indeed it will appear that far as I have grown from my earlier attitudes, I never revolted from them. I am too much an empiricist to have done so. If I had lived in a dream world, that world was as real as are all my dreams in sleep; that is, the dream world was my experience, and an expression of what was most deeply important to me. I now see all of it to be symbolic expression, yet it has never ceased to seem to me an expression of reality. The question through the years has been not whether religious experience is a real experience, but what reality is experienced in it.

So I studied at Harvard as a graduate student in the Divinity School. My work there was interrupted by a year and a half of illness, but I had a year and a half at Harvard before I went on to Oxford to finish my training. At Harvard I studied under one of the few really great groups of scholars America has ever brought together. Ephraim Emerton, G. F. Moore, James Ropes, George LaPiana, Kirsopp Lake, F. C. Conybeare, Charles Gulick—indeed a list of Olympians. Here I was presented with the most exacting scholarship coupled with vivid historical imagination.

PERSONAL

Lake once asked me what was my church, and when I said "Methodist" he only answered quietly, "Never mind. They're no worse than the others."

At Harvard empiricism was at its noblest. No one cared what I believed, but they cared tremendously that I be able to justify by evidence anything I said about historical fact. The difference between the verifiable fact and the theory by which facts might seem related is one of the most important lessons the human mind can learn. I shall never forget an example of it in one of Emerton's lectures. I remember it so vividly, thirty-five years later, that I shall write it in quotation marks:

"The argument for the Papacy as the head of Christendom stands or falls with a *therefore*. Granted that the evidence supports the claim that Jesus founded the church organization and put Peter at its head with the power of the keys (which I do not grant): granted that Peter eventually went to Rome and founded the Christian organization there (for which there is no adequate evidence): beyond this the Church says, 'Therefore the men who happened to succeed Peter as head of the Roman diocese succeeded also to his powers of the keys and to his headship of all Christendom.' The step for which there is no evidence whatever relies upon this *therefore*."

Statements of faith, I learned, are necessary if we are to make any connected narrative out of the fragmentary raw materials of historical records. But these imaginary (imaginative, if you will) lines which connect the points of historical data, the proper historian, like the proper scientist, calls *hypotheses.* And as he is eager, by new evidence or fresh study of old evidence, to correct the connecting lines of others, so he must welcome any correction of his own lines. That is, in these years of the First World War and the new chaos which followed it, I was forced at once to adjust to the finest aspect of the nineteenth century, itself a world I had known nothing of, the world of scientific thinking.

For the contribution of the scientific world is not that it devised the idea of the controlled experiment, tremendous an advance as that was. The techniques of verifying facts differ in all the natural sciences, and historians of the nineteenth century had been just as active in establishing techniques of verification as had the workers in laboratories. Paleography and philological study (in which a passage is dated by its type of Latin or Greek or whatever) are only two of the many substitutes for controlled experiments. The historian wants his facts as pure as any chemist, and tries, in his own way, just as hard to make them so. But facts themselves have meaning only in a context, historical or physical, and the existence and correction of hypotheses is never directly to be proved. So while by imagination and by devising some sort of system of verification, the scientist constructs the context of his facts, by critical reserve he is aware that that context is hypothetical, quite different from the facts themselves. However much he may criticize the theories of his fellows, once a fact is

Personal

fully established he can never disregard it in his future hypotheses. Often in both chemistry and history what had seemed to be a fact turns out not to be so by more accurate study. This discovery in turn becomes a new fact, and woe be to the historian or chemist who disregards it. At any point, however, the scientific thinker is distinguished by his simultaneous loyalty to facts and his critical attitude toward hypotheses or theories, including his own.

In other words, the scientist, quite as much as the historian, deals with faith; that is, unverifiable supposition on the basis of which he must proceed. But all the movement of history and chemistry has been to try to abolish the world of faith and to substitute for it complete knowledge of the universe and of ourselves as facts.

No one is more eager and quick than the scientist to admit that this dream of the modern scientific world is a dream which we are not even approximately realizing. The story of the development of man as told by historians, for example, is still, and presumably will always be, largely a matter of hypothesis and faith. The scientific worker, however, is not content to spend his life teaching the faith he has learned, history as he was taught it, to his pupils. We know a promising student at once when he begins to challenge what he has been taught and to look about for new facts which will make us redraw some of the old lines. The scientific mind is characterized by its lifelong distrust of old faiths and by its delight in getting facts which make new faiths necessary. When this kind of mind attacks an old faith, as when Einstein corrected some of the Newtonian generalizations, everyone is ready to accept—that is, everyone who can understand. But when the historian studies the Gospels, and concludes that much in them is legend and has no claim to be considered as fact (with the inevitable result that new historical lines must be drawn), this seems to be, and is, an attack upon a faith which had become Faith. Here the popular resistance is quite another matter. Not only are great vested interests unsettled, but the very fabric with which man had clothed his nakedness seems to be taken from him.

The impact of all this, fortunately, I felt only gradually. All that I was aware of at first was that here was an atmosphere which fired my enthusiasm as nothing since Uncle Charlie's mysticism had done. There was so much that was positive in it, the possibility of new discovery and evaluation, that I had no notion of the process by which my Faiths shrank to faiths as I learned to hold one or the other of them up to the light of facts. When a man who is not a scholar loses his faith he may have nothing but diversion to turn to in its place.

As I lost the old Faiths, already, like a snake, new skin had grown under them, so that I was never without the protection of an orientation. For the scholar in the field has fresh orientation to life through his active search for new positions in whose value he can have faith. The greatest protection we have from the forces of nature and society, as well as from the inner powers of destruction, is a sense of orientation to what is posi-

PERSONAL

tive, meaningful, and creative. One can be clothed in the search for truth as satisfactorily as in its dogmatic possession.

So, at Harvard and Oxford, I came into a new life. The nearly three years in Europe were of the greatest value in many ways. At Oxford I met no one so stimulating or formative as the great men at Harvard, and I discovered that there was little opportunity for a graduate student there to get much from the older scholars. I spent my time largely in reading in the Bodleian Library, and in writing my dissertation. The most important thing England and the Continent did for me was to isolate me from my parents, from the Methodist church, and from all my immediate obligations to those who represented the old orientations. I made the transition to the new point of view without friction or episode, and, consequently, I did not have to go too far, or strike an attitude of revolt, in order to declare my independence. I still felt the old loyalties, to the point that in the second year abroad I was finally ordained as a Methodist minister in Paris! At the same time I was now so matured that I made enduring friendships with several of my fellow-students, and found no estrangement in any of them. I returned to America so far left (in theology) that none of the seminaries which had led me to hope for a job wanted me, but by one of the happy coincidences of my life I got an instructorship in history at Yale.

Details of the following years would be of no interest here. Externally my life has been the extremely uninteresting one of a scholar who advanced from instructor to professor at Yale, and who since then has had twenty years of the security that a professorship in a great university conveys. Here, as I have taught in various fields, I have been steadily working out the program I set for myself when I went to Harvard, to get what information I could while I slowly transformed what was best from my whole heritage into a pattern which seemed to me to make some sense for living in the new age. Home life and six children, together with the always living problems of my students, have kept me completely in touch with the pulse of life. At the same time, the problems of bringing up a large family on an academic salary, but with the ambitions for them that they have the best possible preparation for life, have made me fully aware of the "realities" which so many people think we professors do not experience. But I have had time to study, read, write, and think. It is in the belief that I have come to some conclusions which may interest others that I write this little book.

2.

DEPTH PSYCHOLOGY: WISH PROJECTION

Even deeper than the effect of historical study upon my thinking has been that of depth psychology, and I am convinced that this is now the greatest problem in religious adjustment for intelligent people.

⸺ Depth psychology is what is more commonly called psychiatry or Freudianism.⸺ It is neither of these, strictly speaking, for both of them are clinical techniques in the treatment of patients who are emotionally or mentally disturbed—the two terms are hard to distinguish. With this, of course, I have had nothing to do directly. But behind these techniques of treatment lie theories, working hypotheses in the sense of the historian and scientist, about the nature of the mind or, more comprehensively, the psyche, and the way it functions. These hypotheses constitute a psychological theory called depth psychology, in spite of the fact that experimental psychologists want to imprison the term psychology within the confines of their own theories and methods. It was this conception which profoundly affected all of us in the twenties and thirties of this century, and which is still the most important thing to face, because at first sight, but only, I believe, at first sight, it seems so devastatingly opposed to religious traditions and attitudes.

I came into an interest in depth psychology through personal friends. The now famous analyst, Dr. Thomas French of Chicago, was my boyhood playmate; and I saw much of him in my twenties and thirties. Through those intense early years when he was working out his own problems, and then being analyzed, we talked of Freud and of psychotherapy for hours and years. To talk thus with Tom was to get as fine a course of lectures on the subject as the world had to offer. After he settled in Chicago I saw him only rarely, but I have carried on my discussions with my sister and with the many psychiatrist friends I made in New Haven. And whenever Tom and I have seen each other in later years, we have continued at once in the old way. I admit also that I have read a few books on the subject.

Freud I never knew, but when Jung was in the United States in 1938, he took deep interest in my work on symbols which was then fully begun. He spent many hours in my study, scrutinizing the material I was gathering, and giving highly stimulating suggestions as to

Depth Psychology: Wish Projection

its meaning. More and more I came to think in terms of the new world of the unconscious which Freud and Jung had opened up. I was never happy with the systematic accounts of psychology given by either of these men, insofar as they can be said to have made systematic accounts at all. And, to my deep regret, I could never afford to be analyzed. But I came more and more to feel the truth of a remark made by a psychologist friend of mine, himself a behaviorist, that in the history of psychology—that is, for the understanding of men, their motives and goals—Freud stood in the same place as Newton in the history of physics. Since history, and even more the history of religion, is primarily a study of man's motives and goals, it seemed to me that we could no longer write or think with the old attitude toward our data.

Depth psychology is so widely disputed and variously explained that a word must be said at the outset as to what I mean when I speak of it. The term itself covers a number of schools of thought, all of which go back to Freud and to his discovery that beneath man's conscious mind is a whole realm of mental activity of which he is not directly aware. What we "have in mind" at any one instant is an infinitesimal fraction of what is in our minds, or what is going on there. Freud divided this great body of activity and material into two sorts. In the "preconscious" mind are memories, things known, which can be "called to mind" at will—as you will instantly do when I suggest that you recall the French word for mother. The chances are very slight that as you read the preceding page you had *mère* "in mind" at all, but it was there just the same—in what Freud called the preconscious.

But all of us sometimes try to remember something which we know perfectly well is in our minds, but it will not "come to mind." Freud demonstrated brilliantly that these failures of memory are often caused by a resentment, a dislike of the object, though he, or anyone else, has by no means explained all cases. Beyond or beneath these forgotten names, dates, incidents, and the like, which we may recall later, lie memories which we do not ever recall. There are languages in which one gets rusty, but which, though they seem almost completely gone at the first attempt to use them, return with great rapidity with a little "brushing up," showing they were there all the while. But if we never "brush them up," they lie all our lives in our unconscious minds. Still deeper memories suddenly return to us in conversation with friends from our childhood, or in associations which are parallel to childhood situations.

Then there are a great number of memories which we never recover at all. They are buried so deep that they seem to rub against that phase of our minds which controls the pulsing of our hearts, the secretions of our stomach and glands, and all the other processes of our physical nature. This deepest dungeon of our memories Freud called the unconscious, and he filled it with all the imprisoned enemies of our security. Terrors, crushing disappointments, frustrations, inferiorities, murderous hatred and impulses, incestuous desires, these threats to our integrity, Freud said, we banish to the unconscious, whose portal is guarded by a special principle which Freud called the censor. And the guard is indeed a thorough one. Most of this repressing is done in early childhood, though the process is vividly apparent in cases when after an accident one completely forgets what happened. The memories of those horrible moments are put as prisoners into the dungeon because they would be too harrowing if we could frequently recall them.

Only in our dreams are we aware of these "repressions," said Freud, and even then the censor rarely lets them come out without heavy disguises. But Freud showed very clearly that these repressed experiences profoundly affect the whole course of our later years, in that they form our tastes, our emotional reactions, and indeed the pattern of our lives. Freud developed his theories in the way any good scientist does—as working hypotheses by which he could explain and control his clinical data. Those data were for him the experiences and desires whose memories he found repressed in his disturbed patients. In the strict family life of Germany and Austria at the turn of the last century he saw human society universally, and the kind of problems which children in this circle had to repress seemed to him and his "orthodox" followers problems which he could recognize in men of all ages and civilizations.

This is not a book on Freudianism, and nothing

short of a book would expound his theories and my reasons for accepting and rejecting what I do. Since I am not an expert in the subject, that is really not important. What I am trying to set forth is the impact this school of thought has had on my ideas of religion.

Actually one of the most important ideas for religion in this type of thinking is the conception called "wish projection." Wish projection is a mechanism by which when we want something very much, it suddenly seems to take shape before our eyes. The simplest manifestation of this is in our dreams, where our wishes take bodily form, and we have adventures with them.

A woman told me a dream she had had—that she was back home as a girl and a suitor was calling; but her father came in and ordered the suitor out. The young man left, slamming the door. I simply remarked to her that I did not know her father was given to slamming doors, and she said yes, that her mother was always scolding him for doing so. The dream was at once apparent. The father was there as himself the suitor, identified by the door slamming, and he was also the censor who drove the suitor out. In both roles the father was a wish projection—both as an illicit object of desire and as the basis for her adjustment to society by banishing the desire.

The last sentence was quite abstract—the kind of thinking we do in the conscious mind. In contrast the thinking done in our unconscious minds is carried on in pictures, or snatches of images, such as the young girl's dream of "Mr. Right," the young man's ideal of his fu-

Depth Psychology: Wish Projection

ture wife, of his true accomplishment in life. Steig's cartoons, "Dreams of Glory," amuse us but make us wince, because we recognize ourselves in them. We may be ashamed of our projections of ourselves as the fireman rescuing the lady at the peril of our lives. Other of our projections, the ideal mother, the ideal man, the true reality, do not shame us at all. Indeed in the figures of speech of poetry, in the heroes of mythology or of fairy tales, we can take open pleasure.

For the process of projection is twofold—one when we do our own image making, as in our dreaming by night or day, or in our creative thinking; and the other when we live in a fantasy presented to us ready made, in a myth, a novel, a play. Sometimes this is done consciously, as an undergraduate told me he did at the movies. He liked to go to westerns, and play the part of the hero throughout, especially at the final kiss. Most of us do this unconsciously. This is the great value of literature, especially novels. The common phrase is that it carries us "into another world." It is escapism, escape from the world of humdrum, anxiety, and pressure, in which we live. What it does is to provide us with ready-made images into which we can project ourselves. The "creative artist" is one who can make his own projections, figures, or personifications, and make them so vividly that unlike us with our dreams, he can record them permanently as novels or paintings or sculpture. These the rest of us can then take as secondhand projections for ourselves.

We accept the projected fantasies of others not only

in the form of poetry, painting, and the novel. We accept similar projections in religion. Religion offers a cultural projection, one formed through the ages and taught to the little child. In accepting it he takes the largest single step to his acculturization. Gradually the dreams of much of eastern Asia have come to settle in the highly complex figure of Buddha, as Jewish civilization centered in Jahweh, and Christian civilizations in Christ and Mary. Into these figures, and many more like them all over the world, have been packed the dreams and wishes of the peoples of these civilizations.

The great religious teachers have been people who projected ideas and figures of the kind that answered the needs of their culture. Like Jesus and the prophets, such teachers have often been rejected by the vested guardians of other sorts of religious traditions. The teachings of the great leaders in religion have endured simply on the pragmatic basis that they, in contrast to the others, projected dreams of God and of right, of the way to spiritual (and physical) security, which really helped the men who accepted them.

Why do I call these teachings about God and the gods wish projection? The idea is by no means original with me. Freud called them "illusions," but this term I would sharply reject. The fact is that no one would have any hesitation in describing figures such as the gods of ancient Egypt and Mesopotamia and Greece and Phoenicia, and Persia and China, to say nothing of the gods of savages, as wish projections. The very ferocity of some of them, like Baal of Syria, who de-

Depth Psychology: Wish Projection

manded that one sacrifice to him one's first-born son, is an asset. This ferocity is just what men want to turn against their enemies, and the reward of sacrificing the first child is that one has many more children afterwards. Good or bad, kind or ferocious, we recognize all these gods as wish projections—all except our own.

But should we, can we, make that exception? I do not think we can. Whether men justify their projection by arguments about the nature of the Infinite or the Absolute, or just believe in God as they have learned about him as children, he still seems to me to be as much a projection in our civilization as among the Aztecs or the Eskimos. This means not that there is no God, but only that all human notions of him are projections. That is why I reject so sharply Freud's term "illusion," which he used for traditional religions, especially Judaism and Christianity. For there is a large measure of truth in many of our projections, while "illusions" implies, like a mirage, that we are experiencing things which do not exist at all except in our own desires.

Actually all scientific theory is projection. Nature knows nothing of the laws of physics as we formulate them; they are convenient projections of our own, convenient because, whatever nature is, these laws help us to adjust to it. Yet they do correspond to reality, though in their own form they are our own imaginative creation. Freud's own psychological theories were "illusions," as much as the religions he thought they supplanted. It remains to be seen whether Freud's formulations are pragmatically more helpful than those of traditional religion. He challenged a dangerous opponent when he called the other formulations "illusions." What I am trying to say is that Freud made a fatal error in implying that his formulations were objectively "true" as compared with other religious projections.

So the first and most profound impact of depth psychology upon my thinking, as, I believe, it is being felt, consciously or unconsciously, among all intelligent people, was to convince me that the supernatural world of God, Jesus, the angels, and all the rest in which I had been brought up, was wish projection. Not all have faced the problem directly and as such, but, repressed in their unconscious minds it is steadily eating away at men's faith, and, I believe, eating away all the more surely because it is eating in secret.

Much of modern man's sense of the futility and meaninglessness of life goes back to the fact that he has really lost faith in the great projected wish of his ancestors, the God in whom they had faith in adversity or prosperity, the one into whose hands they, like Jesus, even in death commended their spirits. We still sing the "Battle Hymn of the Republic," but out of the lowest years of the two world wars our generation could compose no such burst of faith. That is not at all because the people of the United States, at least, were more torn or terrified by the two last wars than were the Americans of the Civil War: the old type of projection has just lost its clarity and compelling power. It was the projection which had given life its form and

Depth Psychology: Wish Projection

meaning, and put all the tragedies of life into perspective. If we recognize that men through the ages have given life meaning largely by projecting wishes of meaning (meaningful gods) upon it and behind it, the great question now is what of meaning is left?

The impact of depth psychology was not only to make me feel that we must be more cautious in talking about men's motives. We must, I saw, recognize that man lives not by his knowledge of right, truth, meaning, and the like, but, basically ignorant of life, by his refusing to believe that life is meaningless even though he does not understand it, and by his projecting a meaning and pattern upon it.

This discovery was to me not paralyzing at all, any more than the discovery of the implications of the historical criticism had been ten years earlier. For if man has always lived on projections he can continue to do so. The trouble is not that our stabilizing ideals and deities are projections, but that we are becoming too self-conscious, too superior in the bad sense of the term, to be ourselves and go on projecting.

The matter of perspective returned to me. We think we see the world about us, that our sight is a true guide to reality. Actually we never see the world as it is at all, but only as the lenses of our eyes arrange it in perspective. A photograph shows us the world as we see it because the camera too rearranges objects by means of its lens. A picture drawn without perspective is accordingly a disorganized mess of detail "without meaning." Yet the fact remains that perspective, or order, is our own projection. It simply does not exist apart from a lens. Is all our vision on that account illusion? By no means. I can throw a ball, or shoot a rifle, in this distorted world of perspective and hit the mark. Two facts then are apparent: first that the world we see is a projected illusion, and second *in the illusion there is a large element of truth*.

The same seems to me to hold about the world of religious projection. Those of us who need to think as experts must develop techniques, as surveyors have done, for isolating the true from the untrue in the illusion. But the rest of us, who are not surveyors, can get along very well in our world of perspective, and will only be confused if the surveyor tries to tell us how he reaches his results, just as we break down when told that Euclidian geometry is inapplicable for astral measurements. This will always be true, so far as I can see. There is no reason why the mass of us should be constantly lectured on the illusory character of our world of perspective, or on the principles of trigonometry, let alone on astral geometry. The business of the surveyor is not to make us all see things as his instruments and mathematics see things, but to give us usable maps, roads, and tunnels. The only reason for my writing this chapter has been, not to throw into confusion those who are living very well with the old formulations, but to reach people who have given up the old and have found no way to create a new projection of meaning into life, man's life on earth and in society. I write not so much to present a new map at this stage, a new pro-

Depth Psychology: Wish Projection

jection, as to suggest the way in which the new map may be made.

Perhaps I can make my point in a parable. Once there was a child who believed in Santa Claus, and loved him. He looked forward to his coming as soon as the days began to shorten. His parents, uncles, and playmates, all the people he knew, talked to him about this wonderful person who would come at the lowest part of the year to bring him gifts. Emulating Santa, the boy learned to save his money to give gifts to his loved ones, and at kindergarten was taught to bring gifts for the poor.

Then his beautiful world and the wonderful person dominating it began to dissolve before his eyes. First a boy of eight laughed at him for believing in Santa; then his own playmates one by one discussed the reality of Santa, always with increasing pessimism. He went to his mother with his question, and for the first time he noticed her eyes shift when she reassured him. After he had gone to her several times with his question she broke down and said yes, the story of Santa is only a story, but it is a true story. She reminded him that Santa was said to come on the day when the Christ child was supposedly born.

Still, she told him, the new light and hope of the world emerges from the darkest days of the year as a new baby is born. The new world is one where men can hope to live and be happy only as they love one another and are kind to one another. Similarly this must be a time of great happiness and love, of giving and receiving gifts to reassure us all of that love. We must not only receive, we must give, just as we must not only be loved but must ourselves actively love.

This is too hard for a little toddler to understand, the mother continued, and so we tell him the wonderful story of Santa. Now you are a big boy, and must learn that the story is really true, even if there is no Santa. For at this time we can all be happy by all being Santas. "I try," she concluded, "to be a Santa with you, your father and your brothers and sisters. You must be a Santa to all of us."

It was a tough lesson for the little fellow, his first approach to abstraction. It took him two years fully to make the adjustment. Being a very unusual child, he took his mother's words deeply to heart, and really learned the lesson of Santa. As he grew older he had to make the same adjustment about the Christmas story itself, but here his mother could not help him, for all her life she believed that story literally. But he was of the new generation, to whom that story also no longer seemed factually true.

We of the intellectual class in this generation must take this next step without a mother to guide us. We must recognize in the old stories the truth which lies behind their story form. We must captivate the values they brought our ancestors even though we no longer project the same types of ideal personalities. This is only in part an intellectual task. The spirit of Christmas we keep alive in ourselves and our homes chiefly

Depth Psychology: Wish Projection

by practicing it and vividly impersonating it. Much that God has stood for in the hearts of our ancestors we can discard, but essentially the conception of God has been a way of teaching the race that love and the other virtues are the only constructive ways of living for the individual and the race. God is no illusion. He is a marvelous form of projection by which we perceive the truth, as is the law of gravity.

For we can now see that this is the way man has always had for perceiving, discovering, the truth. Given a lot of facts, we begin to see a pattern in them. The scientist says: I believe that the pattern is thus and so, and that if I set up such and such an experiment I will get such and such results. If he has thought truly, his experiment comes out as he predicted. But *his thought is still a projection*, which will have to be endlessly corrected, and will always be a human projection.

Most of us have thought in personalities, not in mathematical formulae. So we have the great God of justice in our tradition, and this is as true as the formulae of physics, no more, no less. Whether there is such a thing as the law of gravity, for most of us it seems very silly to debate. It seems to me just as silly to question the existence of God for most people. This is the way the great mass of us approach the truth of ethics, our life with others and with ourselves. And those of us who have come into more abstract thinking miss the person of God as the boy of six aches for Santa. If you, reader, naturally believe in God there is no reason in the world for not doing so. My point is simply that the rest of us are lost if we do not carry the values you find in God into our deepest thought and action.

The fact is, of course, that the rest of us have not stopped projecting because we do not do so in personal form. For belief in the basic values, belief that the values are values, is as much a matter of projection as any other mythology. The fact that we must accept is that human beings live on projections, not on real knowledge at all. We are still human beings in this as in everything else. But through the ages each new civilization has had to make fresh projections, new gods, theologies, moral and social standards. These have had to be in terms meaningful to the new civilization. We are coming into a new civilization ourselves, one in which the old formulations are increasingly meaningless to many of our most intelligent people. In the struggle to work out new formulations the protagonists of the old call this a period of collapse, decline, decadence. But many of us are, like a brilliant physicist of my acquaintance, deeply nostalgic for the religion of our childhood. He said to me, "We don't know where we are going, whether forward, left, or right. Of only one thing we are sure: we cannot go back."

So the troubles of our generation may be decadence and death, but they may also be the birth of a new civilization, according as we have the courage to face the implications of the new knowledge. Of this we can be sure: in the new civilization as in the old, man will live meaningfully only as he lives on his pro-

Depth Psychology: Wish Projection

jections of meaning. If now some of us find it more illuminating to talk about justice than the God of Justice, of liberty than Liberty, then for the sake of all that is holy let us talk of justice and liberty with small letters and practice them. They will be no less projections than were the figures in capitals, and may be no less inspiring than those used to be. What we need is the stabilization and sense of purpose those words have for us. We can use them only as wish projections, but they can still be the plumb line of the foundations of society in the future as they have been in the past, even though we now recognize that they are wish projections.

Do you sneer at projections, calling them dreams and supposing that dreams are illusions, while you want to get down to facts? Life so envisaged is indeed a wish projection. If we call the hopes and ideals of mankind only dreams, then we must face the fact that man can live constructively only as he dreams and tries to live by his dreams. Poetry, theology, physical theory, psychological theory, piety, social and individual values, these are all variant forms in which man projects his theories or dreams upon the great unknown reality which is himself and his environment. The call upon men of the new civilization is that we be adults to a degree no men in the past have had to be. As we have learned more about ourselves, more about the fact of wish projection, we must face up to ourselves as an adolescent has to learn to do.

Not just America is adolescent. The call is clear not only to us but to Englishmen, Frenchmen, and all others, that we must go on into the new adaptations or, by clinging to the old, mark ourselves among the "retarded," those unable ever to come into maturity at all.

Some dreams are "bad" dreams, like fascism and communism; some dreams are better dreams. We must scrutinize all of them by every check we can get, the techniques of psychology, sociology, history, philosophy, and the rest. Indeed it is a tremendous asset that we now know that we think largely in projections, because now we can criticize these as our parents could not. The Calvinist was unable to distinguish what was good and what was destructive in his God, for he had to take the figure as given in tradition. Scrutiny of our projections is possible only as we have learned to recognize them as such.

Depth psychology gives us our great imperative: we must cultivate our projections or dreams, and live by them, even while we admit to ourselves that they are projections. For we are lost without guidance, and much as we may be guided by the experience of the past and the criticisms of the present, ultimately we have no guidance but our dreams. At the same time the new age demands that we critically scrutinize our projections, and never forget that that is what they are.

3

DEPTH PSYCHOLOGY: SYMBOLS

Another radical addition to my thinking from depth psychology is becoming increasingly apparent. It is that our most important thinking is done by those parts of our mind of which we are not aware, and that the processes of that thinking are quite ungoverned by logic in either the older or newer senses. All thinking may use words, but only the formulated thinking of our conscious minds uses words alone. For the rest we use pictures, images, forms, all the stuff that parades before us in our nightly dreams when words are rarely part of the dream at all.

The dream I recounted in the previous chapter had no words—simply a situation of tension between the father as suitor and the father as censor, and the clue to the meaning in the slammed door. But occasionally a word, even an abstract word, will itself be a picture and as such play a part in our dreams.

Some twenty years ago I dreamed that I was a boy in school translating a passage in Greek, but I was stuck, deadlocked, because I could not translate a key word in the passage. I awoke in the horror of nightmare, but only after I awoke did the Greek word itself come to my mind: it was *eleutheria*, freedom. The rest of the Greek passage never was recalled—never had any importance. The dream was concerned with my passionate desire for freedom which shocked the censor, my conscience, into trying to repress it. Provoked by my problems at the time, it was really a dream of a childish situation in which, probably in those intense religious years of adolescence when I was learning Greek, a part of my nature was revolting against my parents and the religious life for which they stood (and probably against learning Greek). The word "freedom" thus stood for a great number of situations or pictures in my life, all put together into this one symbol, the word. Words can play a part in dreams, that is, but rarely arguments, discourses, sentences, and paragraphs.

The terrific labor of composition is to put words together which will actually embody and convey our thoughts. "I know what I want to say, but I can't seem to say it" is the cry of everyone, the master stylist and the poet no less than the yokel trying to write his first love letter. Life has fewer delights greater than the sense of victory when we do at last satisfactorily compose our thoughts in words. But it is too great a strug-

Depth Psychology: Symbols

gle for most of us to try at any length, and even with those who write extensively only a fraction of their actual thinking ever gets organized into verbal chapters. The "right word," the *mot juste,* can become a real object of religion to a stylist.

There are exceptions, people whose verbal facility far exceeds their actual thinking: the constant chatterer, the brilliant conversationalist, the facile writer, even the poet who, as has often been said of Tennyson and Swinburne, can keep the music of the verse going after all thought has been exhausted. But such verbal ease usually thrives at the expense of depth of thought, and freely as some of these people seem to flow in words, most of them slow down or completely falter when they want to say something deeply important to themselves. It was no accident that it took Tennyson seventeen years to write his one really thoughtful poem, "In Memoriam." The few exceptions, such as the incredibly prolific and profound medieval scholastics, or such German scholars as Mommsen, Kant, Hegel, Wundt, and Harnack, must not bother us. Of such is *not* the kingdom of earth. The great majority of us know very well that most of our thinking is not done in words.

This does not mean that non-verbal, or sub-verbal, subconscious thinking is not often excellent thinking. We have all had the experience of waking up in the morning with an answer worked out for a problem which completely baffled us when we tried to solve it consciously the night before. Indeed the whole process by which the clouds of thought are crystallized into verbal snowflakes is one which no one remotely understands. It is certainly largely beyond our control. The point is that most of our verbal vocabulary is only convenient filler and connection for a relatively few words which have deep symbolic importance for us. The word "freedom" which came up in my dream is obviously such a word for me, as it is for most people in our day. But in writing that last sentence all I did was to put a lot of padding about the word freedom so that that word would stand out and impress the reader. The rest of the sentence did not matter. Language is an elaborate machinery of ballistics by which in a barrage of sound, we shoot off a few bullets, the words with deep and real significance.

In all of this the bullet I am trying to shoot is the word symbol. The word "symbol" is itself a symbol for —that is, a convenient way of referring to—the words or forms in which our sub-verbal thoughts are embodied. A great complex of these operate in our lives. There are the little meaningless mannerisms, unimportant in themselves but highly symbolic, by which we recognize a gentleman or a lady in the conventional sense. There are the deeply rooted symbols of our democratic way of life—freedom, a sense of fair play, the right of an individual within limits (whatever that should mean) to live his own life. These symbols are under attack in our age from both communism and those who are using communism as a screen while they throw bombs at personal liberty. There are the symbols of family relations, mother protection, father disci-

Depth Psychology: Symbols

pline, sibling rivalry, as well as the more adolescent symbols of sex. Such are only a few of what I might call "words" from the great symbolic vocabulary by which we live. Some of them are symbolic words or forms which arouse horror or loathing in us. Some fill us with warmth and beauty. Some attract and repel, make us desire and hate them, simultaneously. Some we want with us so that we are protected by them, as we are by conventional clothing, or by an amulet or medal or religious symbol, whatever we call it, with power to bless or protect us.

For however intellectual, scientific, or profound we may be, we all live from day to day by symbols, whose power, whose existence even, we little suspect, and over whose operation in our lives we have very little rational control. We are basically as illogical as a child in my wife's nursery school who so resented his mother's taking his bottle from him at three (why she did it we could not understand) that he refused to drink milk at all. The mother would not yield and give him back the bottle, and so there was a deadlock. My wife suspected that the child really wanted his milk badly, and suggested that the mother put a pink coloring into it so that it would not look like milk. At once all problems were solved. Each had made his point. The boy was not drinking the *white* stuff, and the mother was getting the boy to drink his milk. The boy knew perfectly well that it was milk he was drinking, would watch his mother color it. But so long as he did not have to yield to the symbolic *white*, he was all right.

He had kept true to his symbolic values, which were basically his attempt, through refusing the symbolic white milk, to be guided too extensively by his mother. No white milk meant his freedom as an individual; taking it meant subservience. So he had won his real point when he forced his mother to color it.

Most of our lives are lived on this level. I am not speaking of a physicist or a historian working out the problems presented by his data (though the questions one scientist asks of his data are often different from those another scientist would ask because of differences in symbolic configurations and values in each man). I am rather speaking of the man really living his life—which means his life in his family, in society, and with his students. Many writers of essays or novels are almost entirely guided by their symbolic values, as I am while I write these lines.

Are we then helpless? Have we really lost all freedom, and become automatons guided by symbols whose origin, nature, and demands we do not understand, and cannot control? This seems the least likely conclusion. We largely do live this sort of lives, but there really is something man can do about it. In this he is faced with a fact of nature, and he must approach it as he approaches other facts of nature.

As to external nature, we now talk about controlling it, but this is an overstatement. Man can indeed make a desert bloom with wheat and roses, but only if he has access to water, can make water flow where it did not flow before, so that the desert is no longer a desert. We can now use electricity for the most amazing conveniences, can live in warmth in winter, in light at night. I shall never forget the first village I saw in North Africa where the natives had no illumination at all. At seven when we went past it the village was already in pitch blackness, simply waiting for the sun the next day. What have we done? Are we creators in God's place changing the order of nature to our will? Certainly not. Nature is exactly as it has always been. What we have done is to find out a little about how nature works, and to utilize the forces of nature to our intelligent purposes. So we have light at night, and food in great cities, never against nature, but simply by knowing how to use some of the forces of nature. We are just as much subject to nature as ever, and do not control it. Our freedom to live as we do, however, comes from our understanding how to live with, and utilize, nature.

The same is true in the subjective life within ourselves. We shall never stop living by largely irrational impulses represented to us in symbols. But we have hardly made a beginning in the problem of understanding how these forces within us work and how we can utilize them constructively for ourselves as individuals and for society. That such an approach to the problem is possible is the discovery of the last few decades. It will take us centuries to work it out, for it is much longer and more difficult than the road from Franklin's kite to Edison's electric light. But the ability to utilize the forces within us is the only hope of freedom.

Toward a Mature Faith

Symbols can be discussed and classified in a wide variety of ways. I have no interest in going deeply into the subject here. Mrs. Susan Langer, among others, has done so in her *Philosophy in a New Key,* and I am also trying to get beneath the surface in my technical studies. But it will be convenient to distinguish three sorts of symbols, with no suggestion that this will be an adequate approach to the problem. So I shall speak briefly of the three as individual or private symbols, social symbols, and religious symbols. But in advance I must warn the reader that the distinction among these is only a matter of convenience in classification, since they actually blend most bewilderingly in our lives.

Two examples of private or individual symbols have already appeared. It is clear that no one who has not studied Greek would use *eleutheria* as a symbol in his dreams. It is equally clear that only a person whose father had persisted in slamming doors would use that as a symbol to identify her father. That is, objects, sounds, words, situations, out of our early life become deeply meaningful to us because they carry a whole world of implications with them. The little child who must have a special blanket in order to get to sleep has a symbol of protection which really brings him a sense of security.

Now the particular blanket thus invested with protecting power for one infant would be meaningless for another—who must have his own blanket. Each is a private symbol for the one infant. But it is not a coincidence that both children, and millions with them,

Depth Psychology: Symbols

want a blanket. We all sleep under blankets, and when we have to make some special adjustment, sleep under a rug or an overcoat, we are most of us quite unhappy, because blankets, not a special one but blankets, are what we like to sleep under. The blanket as such has become almost a universal symbol. This transition from private to universal symbols is something we are just beginning to consider. Indeed the Jungian school has been so impressed with the spontaneous re-emergence of primordial and universal symbols in the dreams of individuals who never heard of their ancient or remote existence that a large part of its psychological theory is based upon the phenomenon. All schools agree, however, that it is impossible to go directly from the universal meaning of a symbol to its value for the individual.

Similarly many of our symbols come out of traumatic experiences, or feeding experiences, as did the symbolism of the bells for Pavlov's dogs. We cannot judge that a bell ringing is a symbol of food for all dogs. No more can we be too quick, without knowing much of the individual person's history, to judge the meaning of symbols in his dreams. Symbols on this private level are the business of the psychiatrist trying to understand and help people one by one. Not a psychiatrist, I have only a layman's knowledge of the subject, that is, no knowledge at all. I mention this category only because no classification of symbols has any value which does not include it.

The second important group of symbols includes

the social symbols. It is through these that we show our conformity to the group, so that the group can accept us as one of itself. Society not only demands that we be dressed, but that our dress conform in amazing minutiae. A man wearing striped trousers and morning coat to work at a machine in a factory would be accepted as one of the group as little as a person coming in blue jeans to work in the office of an ambassador. A garage mechanic would not be one of the boys in the garage if he spoke purely in the Oxford manner, just as uncouth grammar would exclude a Harvard professor from the society of his peers. Such a professor might be extremely brilliant in physics, but he would be invited to few Harvard homes to dinner. That is, our ways of speaking and dressing are highly important symbols of our belonging in this or that sort of group. They are usually taken for granted until a real non-conformist comes along—and then the reaction is instantaneous and usually final. A fancy-dress ball releases our inhibitions because a little of this cramping demand for conformity is relaxed and one can go to the ball wearing what is personally, not socially, symbolic. Or rather, society for the moment countenances the personal.

These are by no means unimportant factors in life. A "regular guy" is one who lives by a given code or rule, whether it be the code of a gentleman or the code of the alley gang. Such codes are the glue which holds any society, civilized or savage, together; they are the lubricant by which society can move without cracking. A few social rules are universal, but very few of them.

Depth Psychology: Symbols

The only one of the ten commandments which is universal is that we may not kill members of our own group. The group as a whole, or its despot acting for the group, may kill a member, but one ordinary member may not kill another. A policeman in uniform may treat an individual in ways which would not be tolerated from other individuals: he wears his uniform precisely to show that in this he is not as other men. The right of property, so deeply symbolic of security with us, and which was reflected in "Thou shalt not steal," is not a universal symbol. The Plains Indians of America had a splendid civilization with no thought of private property, so that "Thou shalt not steal" still does not make sense to them as we understand it. What is permitted or not permitted in sexual relations varies enormously in different civilizations.

I do not believe that all ethical variations are interchangeably and indifferently good. To that we shall return. Here I am only pointing out that much of our law, certainly all of our etiquette, is of value chiefly as a symbol that the man who conforms can be regarded as a reliable member of the group. With one who conforms to our code we feel safe, and the feeling is quite reciprocal. The most important part of education, in America, Russia, or the Island of Truk, is to make the little child sensitive to the symbolic demands of his civilization. A new type of social organization, such as was inaugurated by the Nazi or Communist Revolutions, can only threaten adults with intolerable brutality while it puts all its hope of permanency on a newly trained youth. The training is in automatic response to the new symbolic forms of conduct.

Where the symbols of secular society leave off and those of religion begin it is impossible to say with any objectivity. Savages make no attempt at a distinction, for the gods are as much a part of society as any other member. There are special acts of reverence for them, as there are special acts for the chiefs, or for one's parents. The same has been true in our own civilization until very recent times. The distinction between the powers of the secular and the ecclesiastical rulers was sufficiently fought over during the Middle Ages in the upper brackets of society: but the ordinary citizen just knew that he must confess all law-breaking to the priest. If the penalty came from different types of courts for different offenses, that made little difference. Not until the eighteenth century was the secular state really born. And it is not born yet in the minds of those who suppose that God will punish one who does any act considered criminal by civil or common law.

But there are religious symbols in the sense that they have value only for religion. That one should circumcise his child, or have his baby baptized, is prompted partly by a desire to conform to social usage, since these are dedications of the child to the demands of a group, at least in some circles. Neither of them can be called a religious act on the part of the child. But going to church in later years, taking the sacraments, these are acts symbolic of the religious desire of the individual himself. True, all such acts can be, and usually are, infused with some social significance. An undertaker or banker, any businessman, may go to church to increase his business, or a young couple in a strange city may go to church to make friends. I have said already that our categories cannot be taken to have more than suggestive value, since, in practice, symbols so commonly overlap these categories.

To understand religious symbols we must begin with the great and distinctive symbols of religion, and we can leave this problem of the overlapping to more detailed investigation. The great symbols of Christianity, for example, are primarily religious, and only secondarily social if at all. There is the cross, which is inseparable from Christianity. As a Methodist boy I had little use for the objective representation of a cross, and considered a crucifix an idol; not one was to be found in our church. But the cross was a verbal symbol we used constantly, so that it was still clearly active in our thinking. "When I survey the wondrous cross," "At the cross, at the cross, where I first saw the light," such hymns expressed our deepest religious aspirations and configurations. For whether as an object in the hand, or as a verbal symbol, the cross demands that we die as Christ died. He died for us, but we appropriate, or are made eligible for, the benefit of his death only insofar as we in some way share in his death, die ourselves. Christianity is by no means unique in presenting its believers with a dead god as its basic symbol. For thousands of years the mummy of Osiris had the same place in the lives and hopes of Egyptians as has the crucified

Christ with us. In this death we shed our old guilt, and are prepared to "rise with Christ," to come into eternal, divine, life.

That is, the symbol of death is our hope of life. We have indeed in this got about as far as possible from logical thinking. The religious impulse on its deepest level has always said *Credo quia absurdum,* "I believe by virtue of the fact that the idea is absurd." Men believe in the absurdity of getting life through a dead person precisely because the object of religion is to heal the cleft within us by which we at once compel ourselves to punishment, continuous punishment, for our sins, while we crave a happy and unending life at the same time. The religious symbol must gratify both these cravings within us, and the best way of doing that, apparently, is to represent the death through which we may hope for life. Is this idea or emotion? Actually it is an emotion produced by two conflicting and incompatible ideas. The theologian tries to reconcile these by means of verbal logic. The great majority of men reconcile them with and in the symbol.

Another religious symbol is the nursing mother, the mother who gives her son life by his birth and by her milk. Medieval representations of the Virgin often showed Christ in her womb, while others showed him actually nursing at her breast. Both these have been given up, and the mother now simply holds the child in her arms, but our minds still see that the child has come from her womb and is fed at her breast. Our minds do so, but rarely our conscious minds. The sym-

Depth Psychology: Symbols

bol is now presented in softened form. Here again, however, the idea at the bottom is the attainment of new life, divine life. We Protestants, who have no use for a figure of the Virgin in our churches, have the verbal symbol in its place. One can almost say that in the very proportion that people reject the formal symbol they put fresh emphasis upon the verbal symbolism of re-birth. We are to be born not of the flesh but the Spirit (as Christ was begotten by the Spirit). The union of divinity and humanity presented in the baby Christ gives us hope that we human beings may come into a share of divine virtues and powers, indeed of divine existence with God in heaven. As he came down and then went up, we who are now down may go up if we are born of the Spirit.

Again all of this is not at all in the conscious mind of the Catholic before an image of the Virgin and Child, but it is an idea deeply felt, and expressed as he reveres the image. It was certainly expressed directly in our Methodist hymns, and will be found just as clearly in the Advent Hymns of the Anglican church. And yet either a Catholic or a Protestant who reads this paragraph may find the idea too crudely stated here. It goes much better in symbolic forms, or in hymnody. But these symbolic expressions have power because they express an idea, one with deep emotional power in their lives, but still an idea.

For the fact is that the basic ideas by which we live are too unsettling for us to face them directly. The most basic idea of all is that we are born naked and helpless in a world we little understand. Most of our rules of civilization and symbols of religion, in form or words or ritual, are designed to conceal from us this deeply disturbing fact, while they give us a sense that the great mystery of life and the great formlessness of the incomprehensible in nature are swallowed up in victory. If we wear the right clothes, belong to the right group of fellow-men, and have a deity who gives us the security of a greater life, we may forget or repress our fears, our shame at our nakedness and inadequacy, and live with security.

The individual can rarely work all this out for himself. The mass of men have no personal judgment or curiosity about universal problems. They will bristle with personal prejudices and symbols in matters which have to do with their relation to their parents, wives, or children, or to the policeman who stops them when speeding. But their relations with the state in general they learn from their party, usually their father's party, and they guide their notions of and relations to God by the teachings of their church, usually their father's church.

In doing so in the past they have had the help of the intelligentsia. Still up to a hundred years ago the best minds of each generation went into law and the church, and gave proper judgments or sermons to establish the laymen in the traditions of their civilization. This is probably still largely true in Catholic parochial schools and colleges, but not elsewhere. The mass of men who have always followed the leader find that

Depth Psychology: Symbols

their leaders are increasingly content with personal solutions, less and less moved by a sense of responsibility for leadership.

The masses now see their leaders rejecting the traditional by not going to church and by preoccupation with science as science, with literature as literature. The leading poets and scientists alike now speak languages quite unintelligible to the masses, and rather pride themselves in doing so. The masses then have left only the representatives of orthodoxies of the past in religion, and demagogues in politics. Most men know just enough to be aware that this is inadequate, but they do not know what to do about it.

What do the great scientists and writers live by in their homes and with their friends? Certainly they do not live there by their abstruse mathematics, or verbally musical lines. Actually the ordinary man would find that these people live quite uncomplicated lives, and have a very simple symbolic vocabulary. The same is true of my most abstract metaphysical friends. Successful personal living can be done on no other basis than the symbolic.

This is why the average man nods when a preacher says that the foundations of human life in society are being destroyed by the scientist. The scientist (and the artist who no longer speaks to mankind but to fellow-artists) thinks such statements are nonsense. But they are not nonsense, for the average man only sees the intelligentsia retiring from traditional codes and symbols to go into worlds forever beyond him. What is the matter with the traditional codes and symbols, the mass of men want to know, and they are given no answer. So their faith in the traditional, and the security that faith gives them, are lost.

The great mass of us need not a new metaphysic, but symbols in which we can again have faith. Whatever need for the new geometries was felt by those who went into astral physics, the mass of men still now, and apparently always will, live in the Euclidian world of three dimensions. If the Euclidian geometry is not universally applicable, so what? For building our houses and bridges it answers as well as ever. So it is in our personal lives. We must still live by simple symbols which put the mystery of life into workable terms for us. I see no reason why we should become futile because we now are aware that our symbols are just that, any more than I feel that the average architect must stop designing houses because he cannot correct his calculations by astral geometry.

In the rest of this book, accordingly, I shall discuss the symbols which I live by, and give some of the rationalizations by which I justify myself in doing so. One who knows men will not be surprised that the symbols are the basic ones I learned from my parents and my Uncle Charlie. I shall quote Scripture to beautify, not justify, my position, and to bring out the fact that though my explanations for their value may not be what I learned from tradition, the value of the symbols seems to me to be unaltered. If the symbols I discuss are verbal rather than forms to be represented in paint or stone,

Depth Psychology: Symbols

that is because I was brought up in a Protestantism which, for all my work with form-symbols, has made them essentially foreign to my personal experience. What I go on to present, that is, is adequate only for myself. There is more here than some would need, less than others. I write largely not because I want people to accept my own pattern of symbols, but because I believe deeply in my method for anchoring my symbols in the new world of scientific, historic, and psychological thinking.

4

FAITH

In discussing symbols which seem to me valuable for the new age I shall discuss largely the old symbols. This is not strange at all, for it is what men have been doing through the ages. Take, for example, a formed rather than a verbal symbol. There is no more vital a symbol for contemporary religion than the cup containing the divine fluid available for men, represented or offered as an actual cup. This symbol can be traced not only to early Christianity, but to the followers of Dionysus, and even to early Mesopotamia. In the form of a vase it was one of the most important symbols for the ancient Egyptians. Each new civilization took the old symbol, and adapted it in terms of accounts of God which were meaningful for it.

A new symbol cannot be custom made. The Nazis in Germany and the Fascists in Italy simply took over

Faith

very ancient symbols and gave them their new meaning. I doubt very much if the design of the American flag meant much to people during the Revolution. It was arbitrarily made, thirteen stripes and thirteen stars for the thirteen states constituting the new nation. We have finally settled on the thirteen stripes and a star for each state—but I do not believe the details even yet mean much to us. Certainly a person in the newer states would get little thrill from seeing that we have thirteen stripes. For the fact is that the original details have largely lost their meaning, and when we now see the flag it simply means to us the United States as a unit.

Similarly the history of the three crosses which constitute the Union Jack is of no importance except to antiquarians. Put together originally to mean that England, Scotland and Ireland had become united, it came to stand for the British Empire. Now that the Empire has become the British Commonwealth, the Union Jack is that Commonwealth in perceptible form. For Britain to discard the Union Jack and adopt a new symbol now that the Empire has become the Commonwealth would be a terrible mistake. What must gradually be done is to read the new entity, the new meaning, into the old symbol. To some ultra-conservative Englishmen the Union Jack still means the old Empire which they cannot believe is gone forever. They want to go "back" to the old meaning of the symbol.

In religion exactly the same problem presents itself. There were pagan martyrs for the old meaning of the symbols whom Christianity had to liquidate, as Merejkowski has so beautifully described in *The Death of the Gods*. Those who think we can no longer go "back" to the old symbols in the forms and words which Christianity presented to us in our childhood, must come to see that we want not new and artificially made symbols, but new meaning from the new world for the old symbols.

We shall of course add a few new ones, as Christianity did in replacing ancient paganism. Such symbols will come to us, however, not by special mail order but by custom and usage, so that they will have taken on symbolic value for us long before most of us recognize that they have done so.

The skeptical and critical attitude, for example, is our approach to truth, our mystic exercise to bring us into perception. As such, seemingly the enemy of religious attitudes, we must now recognize in it only the enemy of the old religious attitude of credulity to creeds. The official attitude of Christianity is *Credo ut intelligam*, I believe in order that I may understand. Very good—this has worked for a millennium, and is still working with a large proportion of our contemporaries. The attitude of the new age, however, is *Dubito ut intelligam*, I doubt in order to understand.

The *Credo* approach made man feel that he understood the ultimate problems of God, nature and man. The *Dubito* approach has shown that much of that understanding was fallacious. Man's doubts seem to be leading him into a new understanding, if not of God, then of nature and of himself. Whatever the creedalists

Faith

say of the doubters, doubting is the ritual for apprehending the truth practiced by the intelligentsia, and they can use no other. Very well, let us doubt that we may understand. If this is our new symbolic ritual, let us practice it.

Actually we shall still be having faith, faith in the ritual of doubt. The change is not so great as it at first appears. Still we believe in order to understand, but believe in the new method rather than the old creeds, theology, and metaphysics. There will still be the outsiders. For as the pagans scorned the new objects of faith of the Christians, traditional Christians will scorn the new faith in doubt. This must discourage us no more than it did the early Christians. Every advance in civilization has had to begin with what seemed to be the destruction of the old. Gothic architects could no longer create in the Romanesque forms, Renaissance architects no longer in the Gothic, and so on down to the present when rejection of what people have been doing is still the starting point for the creative architect. It is so in painting, in literature, in all the arts. It is so in life. The older generation always thinks the younger is decadent because the living impulses of the young people make them begin with revolt and doubt. What the older generation thinks of the younger is really not important. All that matters is that the young find themselves by doubting their predecessors.

We must doubt our predecessors. But it is time for us to recognize at last that we are doubting not the ends of our predecessors but the means by which they wanted to reach those ends. Still the end of the artist is to paint a picture which will express his sense of form and color values. Still the poet wants to set in musical cadence the deepest thoughts of his heart. Always the architect wants to build a structure which will be both serviceable for the ends desired, and beautiful to look at. With us, in the matter of religion or the human quest, the end still is *ut intelligam,* that I may understand. Our doubting is only that the acceptance of a creed is the best way to get understanding. We think we have a better method, that of doubt. At least, like any other school of artists, we must proceed in our own way. We cannot be anything but hollow echoes if we take the methods of past civilizations.

We find ourselves at once in one of the many paradoxes we shall encounter—that doubt is, at least for us, so important a means to truth that we must have faith in it. The man of our generation who is in real trouble is the one who has lost faith in doubting. His doubting is no longer productive, but has become akin to the psychopathic doubt of the depressive, in which there is no faith. Such a man must go "back" to faith in some creed, or break down altogether. The person who has begun doubting a creed, but is afraid of his doubts, similarly is in trouble, and will be so until, consciously or unconsciously, he begins to have faith in his doubting. Then only can doubt lead to creativity.

So there abide with us faith and doubt; but even for the doubter the greater of these is faith. The first

Faith

of the old-new symbols or symbolic attitudes in religion which I want to discuss is, accordingly, faith. We shall see that to live successfully we must have faith in much more than our doubts.

In contrast with animals, man needs more than physical comfort and survival for himself and his kind. He needs also a sense that he understands his environment and himself, his obligations, the right way, which basically is the successful way, to live with his fellows, and what he should expect from his fellows.

Animals die, but, so far as we know, they have no such abstraction as "death" to bother them while they are alive. The fluctuation of the seasons is a practical problem to squirrels and bears, one for which they make elaborate preparation or adjustments. But I doubt that adequacy or lack of rainfall, the cycles of crops and seasons, the terror of lightning and thunder, the origin of life, or the difference between the animate and inanimate ever make them ask "Why?"

Without debating just how far such problems exist for other forms of animal life, it is safe to say that they are basic for human beings. The dawning of intelligence in a three- or four-year-old child is marked very much by his early learning skills to walk and climb and manipulate objects with his hands, but, as a human being, even more by his asking questions about himself and natural phenomena. "Where does the rain come from?" "Where do babies come from?" "Why are the days longer in summer?" "Where is Grandma now that she is dead?" "Who made the world?"

We do not know at what stage in his development man began to ask such questions, but apparently they marked the beginning of human intelligence in the past, as they still do in a baby. It is quite wrong to dismiss these questions in a child with the mature answer of agnosticism, "We do not know but are trying in science to find out." The great majority of us do not have to have the right answers to such questions, but we do have to have the satisfaction that we, or at least that experts, know the answers.

Answers to all important questions are myths, and, as I have said, we all live by myths. A child brought up in a world which he thinks was made by a kind and loving personality called "God" lives in a much more secure world, and hence will develop much more security within himself, than a child put off by his parents without answers at all. Even such myths as the stork and the doctor's black bag are better than no answers, or vague answers, to his questions. Granted that myths often give only an illusion of understanding, as human beings we must have our myths.

Just how at the dawn of intelligence man answered those questions we do not know, but very early he must have begun to answer them with myths, since every race of people lives in a cushion of myths, and must so live. I once knew a little boy of three who sat quietly through a particularly savage thunderstorm, but suddenly announced: "I know what makes a thunderstorm! Jesus was going upstairs with a bucket of water. God was coming downstairs with a lighted candle. They bumped into each other on the stairs. God dropped the candle, and that made lightning. Jesus dropped the bucket of water, and that made rain. And the bump made the thunder." I have often wondered what became of that little chap, whose name I have long since forgotten. Certainly he had a creative mind, because he faced the unknown not with terror but with imagination. I doubt that he ever became neurotic, since, when he did not know, he had power to make a myth.

All of the security and confidence of early men came to them through confidence in their myths, and the rituals of protection which grew out of the myths and themselves suggested myths. The savages on the islands of the Pacific have learned to make excellent boats, but they do not dare launch a boat which has not been made by people skilled in the magic rituals of boatmaking. Otherwise, the spirits of wind and wave will bring certain disaster. Some of the myths can be told at length by the "old man" of a tribe, but other myths survive only unconsciously or implicitly in savage forms of verbal expression or of ritual.

Some kinds of myth account for the particular—the dryad in a special tree; the numen, as the Romans called it, or the vital spirit, of a valley or mountain; the protective value of a horseshoe or a rabbit's foot. With these go myths of the wholeness of nature, of creation, man's origin, his relation to animals, and the like. The unpredictable takes form and becomes manageable, endurable, when it is called luck, good or bad, even more so when it is made into a goddess whom we can call "Fortuna." With this formulation the human spirit can face the unexpected. We can live with our more successful neighbors when we can say "He had all the luck," and accept our own failures when we say "I just did not get the breaks." Or, if Luck is a person, or quasi-person, we can come to grips with it by wearing proper charms, saying lucky words, all such ritual as emerges in crap games.

Special myths of the weather, the sea, the seasons, love, health, war, these have given most people a welter of gods. At the same time there may be, usually is, an over-all myth by which everything is unified in a single Creator and Ruler. These two kinds of myths usually live comfortably side by side. Very few people even today try to work out a single myth to which everyone and everything is secondary. The philosophers have been doing this for thousands of years without the general victory of any one philosophy. We have our Christian ethics and our business ethics and our country club ethics, to say nothing of the code of a gentleman. The majority of "upper class" people believe in all four of these, each as a final entity, to the point that they quite resent a rector in their church who demands that the other three be made subservient to Christian ethics. True, the myth behind the others is implicit, not put into a story, while the stories of the foundations of

Faith

Christian ethics are explicit. But most of us pay only lip service to the notion that there is a single over-all system of ethics.

If this is true, we may regard polytheism with fresh eyes. Polytheists tell stories of the one great God, or the Father of the gods, but also stories of all the particular gods. They will insist, like Homer, upon the supreme power of Zeus while they show the other gods cheating and getting round his commands all the while. Very few Christians refuse to wish themselves and others good luck: because implicitly, in the minds of Christians, luck is a power alongside God. I once went fishing with Uncle Charlie who told me that God was going to give him a fish, and when he caught it repeated that God had given it to him. But that is the language of few Christian fishermen. It would seem irreverent to them. The Great God is reserved for special moods and occasions when we seem to ourselves to face the universal and ultimate. When it comes to catching a fish, we feel much more comfortable talking about luck.

Polytheism is almost universally practiced along with worship of a universal God because men have particular problems more often than universal ones. The Catholic saints, with their special powers, are an explicit manifestation of the need for particular and immediately applicable intervention and control. St. Christopher was the direct protector of the soldiers, to the point that in the last war Protestants and Jews in great numbers went to the Catholic chaplain for his medals to wear. In the Civil War, stories were told without number by people of both sides about soldiers who had been saved by carrying a New Testament in their pockets over their hearts. Any other book would, physically, have done as well, but the stories were all about a pocket Testament which, implicitly, had a direct power not found in other volumes.

I was brought up in practice a tritheist, for whom the three Persons of the Trinity were united only vaguely into monotheism. To this I added a personal devil, always, with his attendants, to be reckoned with. Martin Luther threw his inkwell at the devil when he came into Luther's study. Jews, by which I mean most Jews, had, along with their monotheism, a mass of spirits good and bad (the most famous bad one was Lilith), and the Moslems have the same. In fact, very few people have been pure polytheists in that they had no idea that a Great Spirit existed above the particular spirits; and very few have been pure monotheists in that they really thought of everything as being under the direct control of a single personality or power.

Social problems I have alluded to, implying that the various codes of ethics are forms of myth. Actually only rare individuals, rarer than they themselves admit, make ethical decisions without reference to some sort of code of "Right." If many moderns insist on spelling the word with a small letter, and talk of ethical relativism, they really capitalize it by their basic loyalty to their own code. Most of us would be driven mad at the suggestion that we create moral values each for himself, and that every other man has the right to do so. From

Faith

early times man has been able to create a society, and accept its limitations, just as he has believed that he had a code given him by a divinely inspired Moses or Lycurgus, or by a divine king, as in Egypt and Persia. Right and wrong, if we are to accept a distinction between them, cannot be arbitrary creations of our own. The code of a caste, like the code of a gentleman, can be taken as ultimate with only implicit mythology, but the myth is there. As to this particular myth, Lord Chesterfield only made the implicit explicit when he said that he had no fear of the final judgment, for God was a gentleman and would know a gentleman when he saw one.

Another form of the myth for the sanction of ethical codes was the Greek belief in the Furies, who visited with terrible punishment those who broke the basic laws of Greek ethics. Plato dreamed of a society under the control of a man who could perceive the universal Right and interpret it as laws for men. Even in our society, that man will be elected President who can be built up, at least during the campaign, to the point where he seems to have similar power. Society could not exist without a social myth, or the individual without a sense, a myth, of Right.

Modern science has invaded this world of myth. We now talk of evolution instead of divine creation, by which we have substituted a new term implying for most of us who are not biologists almost as many blind spots as the old. Biologists can go much farther with the investigation of phenomena under the theory of evolution than under that of creation, but as an over-all theory in the popular mind it is really a new myth, it is a term which in general gives a quite fictitious sense that we understand man's place in the universe. Plato called a myth a "likely story." Modern science has techniques for testing the relative likelihood of some of our stories, but when it comes to comprehensive accounts, evolution is an example of the fact that we still find our adjustment through likely stories. Take it away. Take away creation too, and let us try to admit that we have really no idea how man came into existence in this universe of flying electric particles. The effect is devastating, intolerable. The mind at once begins groping for new myths to take its place.

Man's private life is something just as confusing to us. One's relation to one's wife which, however deeply based on the sex urge, has come to involve so many other things, is utterly different from the relation of sexes among animals. It involves an elaborate code of rights and duties. Anthropology shows us how widely varied these mythical codes of marriage are in different societies. But each society has to treat its own code as Right, and is thrown into utter confusion when it begins to question that Right. A large part of modern confusion in personal life comes from the fact that our traditional codes of marital relations are now being challenged. The demands of women for freedom from the traditional status of "housewife," while they still feel the old need of a husband, children, and the social dignity of being a wife, put many modern women in psychological chaos. And their husbands no less. What is lost is a clear myth by reference to which all such matters can be settled. The great number of happy homes today are those which still have a clear, if unformulated, myth of the Right in such matters. Mohammedan women, shut up in the women's quarters, can keep their sanity and live ordered lives, insofar as they accept that sort of life for themselves and their daughters as the Right, as do the great majority of Mohammedan women I have seen. Married happiness does not come from having the right code so much as from believing that the code one has is Right. But every code is a mythical code.

The same is true of the social structure in which we meet our fellows, and bring up our children. Modern society regards with incredulity the structure of the older societies, those of Europe or India, in which social stability was guaranteed by the myth that God has been pleased to put us each into one or another level of society, and that, while each has the rights and duties of that level, the capital sin is to challenge one's place in society, and to refuse to recognize the superior rights of one's superiors, or claim them for oneself. A friend of mine repeatedly alludes to his grandmother, who was a recognized aristocrat and was always treated as such; she knew her place in society and everyone else knew it. He contrasts this with the problems his own wife has with servants and tradespeople. I am far from

Toward a Mature Faith

sharing his nostalgia for this social myth; I simply point out that in the present chaos of social mythology, man is made deeply unhappy.

The way to social adjustment is to find a myth, a sense of Right, accept it, and live by it. You may use the old terms of gentleman or lady, or the term popular in schools, "rules of the game," or have no term at all, though you will do better with terms. But a myth of the structure of society and of your place in it is an essential for happiness, whether you have ever formulated the myth or not. It is most interesting that these myths exist largely in the unconscious mind and are rarely formulated. A "gentleman" would be incensed at being requested to formulate his mythical code. But it exists none the less surely as a guide for himself and as a criterion for judging others. Emily Post has written a Bible for the American code of manners, which she, like Moses, only codified from the manners of "Right people." The existence of such "Right people" is a mythical concept if ever there was one, but if my daughter wants a formal wedding I shall have to buy a copy of that Bible, or I shall feel terribly insecure and unhappy at the wedding.

The myths of social organization which we call government or the state, the myth of obligation, even to giving one's life for the state, are no less essential for man's stability. I belong myself to the democratic tradition which believes that the state is only a legal fiction, and that the reality is the individual. I have no use for over-all totalities which claim precedence to the indi-

Faith

vidual, whether they present themselves in fascist, communist, or ecclesiastic forms. Yet in practice, when I see the courts, the legislative assemblies, the legal tradition, the police uniform (not always the policeman), the Army and its right to draft me or my sons, the tax collector, I must fall back upon the state as a reality, with real powers over me as an individual. That is, I accept a myth again.

By this time I hope the impression is being made that, as I am using the term, "myth" is by no means a word for something untrue or fictitious, as when we contrast the "true" and the "mythical." A myth is man's way of piecing together the tattered ends of experience and knowledge into a connected whole to which he can adjust himself. Or it is a way to stabilize oneself in a sense of Right. The function of science, natural science, social science, psychology, is to increase man's knowledge of reality. It will always be a threat to established myths, because the new discoveries cannot be restricted to old conventions, and are usually of a nature to require adjustments of mythical thinking. But they, or science itself, give us only shreds of knowledge and so do not replace at all the need for myths. Still we must have the illusion that we know truth and the Right, consciously or unconsciously, if our lives are to seem to us to have any form or purpose—if our lives, as we say, are to have "meaning."

The term which Christianity used for this acceptance of over-all accounts is "faith," which meant in early days a fixed acceptance, a stability. God alone has true faith, said the ancients, because God alone has true stability, is the unchanging. Insofar as a man has faith, in our own terms faith in an over-all account of nature or Right, he has stability, and I know no other way by which man can hope to get stability.

The danger of faith is that it produces smugness, and intolerance of challenge or question. We come then into another presentation of the basic paradox of life. Stability can go only a little way before it becomes rigidity and bigotry, and must be spaded up with doubt arising from fresh perceptions of reality. Here is the new faith again, our faith in doubt. The value of this spading I would not minimize. A large part of my own life has been devoted to the spade. It has been so because I fully accept the myth that knowledge is better than ignorance, that old accounts must be constantly corrected, that elasticity is better than the closed mind, though I could not demonstrate that one of these statements is true. But my life has been stabilized, even in spading, by the belief in the value of spading. At the same time, when I leave my study to live my full life, I have to be stabilized by social and personal faiths which give a sense of value and meaning to my pattern. For man lives by myths, by faith in myths, and we simply are trying to fool ourselves when we suppose we can live in any other way.

Shall we be solid or fluid, then? The answer is we must be both. The important thing for the modern man to discover is that he *may* be both, for the modern intel-

FAITH

lectual, in priding himself on his fluidity, his openmindedness, has inevitably led himself into a sense of purposelessness, meaninglessness, vagueness. He has robbed himself of the only way life can have meaning as a whole. One function of intelligence is to challenge the old myths. An equally important function, in historical terms a much more important function, is to make life livable by the formulation of creeds and codes, both of them myths, on the basis of which we can face life with stability. However much we doubt, and have faith in doubt, we must have creeds and believe in them, even while we are ready to modify them as new facts make modification seem advisable.

For nothing seems clearer to me than that life has meaning only as we give it meaning. I would not deny that there is a true Right, what used to be called a Natural Law or a Divine Law for man. But it is obvious that nature itself, or the scientific study of nature, does not tell us what this Right is. All formulations of the Right have been human creations, however much men in different civilizations have constructed myths of revelation to guarantee the truth of their moral and scientific traditions. In discovering this, modern man has come to the staggering conclusion that all codes and stories by which life is given meaning are "relative," that we have no access to the true Right. Many men have even denied that such a thing as the true Right exists at all. They have made themselves self-conscious and faltering about giving life a meaningful pattern, and have saved themselves, when they did so, by unconscious adherence to a code of right, or by a myth of the value of research.

But we are still human beings, and cannot carry on without a conscious or unconscious sense of meaning. In no biological laboratory will we ever find a meaning for life, as we use the term on the human level. We must create that meaning in ourselves, and then have faith in it, to live successfully. Our children will question our faiths if they are intelligent, but will in the end have to form faiths of their own, which in the continuity of a given civilization will usually differ from ours only in details. "The just shall live by faith." That is, those who are stable will live by accepted over-all patterns. This is as true now as when Paul said it.

How shall we go about creating myths in which we can believe? Can we lift ourselves by our own bootstraps? The first way to do so is by looking at the experiences of life and drawing conclusions about them. This chapter is itself a direct example of what I mean. For that life is a paradox of stability and fluidity, that man lives by faith in myths, that this is the stabilizing factor, that life has meaning only as we give it meaning, each of these is a mythological statement which some of my readers will accept and give faith to, and which others will reject. Those who reject my myth will either go on to use the same method but come to different mythical conclusions, or will reject my whole thesis in the interest of traditional myths in which they still have faith, such deep faith that they cannot call them myths

Faith

at all. What I am trying to say is that we have not gone so far from the latter group as we had supposed. In the older formulations of Christian tradition there was much truth. For example, we have just found, perhaps, deep truth in Paul's insistence that the just shall live by faith. To this we can return with satisfaction, since Paul, as we shall repeatedly find, was a profound psychologist.

I have just said that it is the function of children to criticize the myths of their parents, but they will usually in the end alter them very little because of the great force of inertia in human life which produces what I call the continuity of civilization. We cannot hope to depart in more than details from the traditions of our fathers. There is no myth less well founded than that individuals or any generation as a whole can start from the beginning and create values, a pattern of life, wholly anew. To sit down and create a new code of sex, of objectives for one's children, of patterns for directing them (or refusing to direct them), of business ethics, of the proprieties and courtesies of social relations, to do all of these *de novo* is utterly beyond the powers of any one human being. Even Aristotle began his description of the ideal state by collecting a score of actual constitutions. True, we may become so engrossed with a passion for painting or music, an overriding ambition in business or the state, that traditional morality and its codes will fade into complete unimportance. We may flout the moral principles of our fathers as violently as does a harlot or a racketeer, or as Hitler did, but there are traditional patterns or myths of life for rationalizing even these aberrations, traditions to which such people make constant appeal.

The great majority of "decent" citizens conform to what tradition has called law and decency, and try, on the whole successfully, to make their children conform to it. Otherwise, any civilization would collapse. These are the roots of the individual, and we dig up our roots at our peril. Actually we who dig up our roots at all dig them up only one or two at a time.

It would be simply impossible for me to decide that I would live by the pattern of an Indian Brahman. Perhaps I could approximate such a change if I went to live in India and cut off all relations with Americans or Europeans. But I doubt if I could do so even then to the conviction of other Brahmans. Science advances only as each new scientist orients himself with the science of the day, which means with the science of the past, however recent. Even more, in the development of civilization we change only very slowly. "One step enough for me" is not a pious wish, but the limitation of humanity at any time.

In view of modern natural sciences, of history, of anthropology, and of psychology, our generation has given up the idea that revelation, at least in its traditional form, lies behind our codes of law and ethics. This is a long step indeed, one which makes us see many things in new perspective. We may no longer believe that God wrote "Thou shalt not kill" with his own finger on a piece of stone. We may regard that

Faith

story as a myth sanctifying a much older tribal rule against killing (i.e. killing within the tribe, of course). Yet we have not on that account become freely murderous, and actually, except under Hitler, Mussolini, and Stalin, we have less tolerance for the killer than did our ancestors. The age-old values of personal truthfulness, the sanctity of a promise or agreement, genuineness, are now as important as ever, and indeed, through such laws as the Pure Food and Drugs Act, are probably better observed than at any time in the past. The fact that we may have abandoned revelation does not mean that we have the slightest idea of giving up our active, if not conscious, faith that the values that our ancestors thought revealed at Sinai are fragments of the Right.

Less obvious is our continuing to observe seasonal festivals. Those who have abandoned any belief in the traditional Christmas story are no less apt than believers to send Christmas cards, put up a Christmas tree with lights and imitation fruit (the glass balls), and things to eat. Whether or not we reject Christianity, we give Christmas gifts, and make it wherever possible a special occasion for the children, when the adults themselves return to the spirit of childhood. Easter is an occasion for identifying ourselves with the new hope of the life of spring by getting new clothes and hats for ourselves and wives and children. The eating of a special meal with eggs, and the old fertility symbol of the bunny, belong to those who do not believe in the resurrection of Jesus as much as to those who do. It is true that the proper preparation for this in the austerity of

Lent is less generally practiced, and on the whole that is a pity.

These, and many other observances in the "Christian Year" that have come down to us are by no means to be given up, for they have a power to give form and meaning to life quite beyond our power to explain them. One either observes Christmas or hates it, for its loss gives one at Christmas time as much a sense of vagueness and meaninglessness as its observance does the reverse. Belief in the story is quite secondary to taking on its spirit, which is as true from the point of the believer as from that of the skeptic. Whether Scrooge was a believer in the Christian story it never occurred to Dickens to include in his "Christmas Carol," and has not seemed important to the faithful who have delighted in it for a century. For the point of the story is that Scrooge, in succumbing to the spirit of Christmas, became a new man with a freshness and vitality he had never had. To have pointed up the Christian story of the origin of Christmas would have narrowed, not broadened, the Carol's appeal for everyone. For Christmas is the spirit of Christmas, however much in practice that spirit may be commercialized. Christmas was celebrated long before the story of the birth of Jesus was told to justify it at all, and still has its meaning in the doing and sharing, a belief far deeper than an acknowledgment that the story of the Virgin Birth is historically true.

That story will seem to us to have great values also when we come to talk about the Christian stories. Here

Faith

I am only saying that one of the best ways to give ourselves form and to fill life with meaning is to accept the basic traditions of our society, its moral traditions, its legal traditions, and its seasonal festivities, for if they all are based upon myths, they in general have truth and formative power for us which it is silly to abandon just because we cannot explain them in terms of controlled experiments or historical documents. It is not that we are safer if we conform, or that life is more pleasant for those accepted by society than for those who feel themselves rejected. Rather it is that in the deeper virtues of kindness, integrity, respect for one another, which are the basis of law and ethics, and in the act of identifying oneself with the seasonal festivities, life gets a sense of form and meaning not otherwise to be achieved.

What is the meaning of life? I cannot say. Does it in itself have any purpose or meaning? We do not know. How may we put meaning into life? For this, perhaps we have begun to see, we must have faith in our imaginations and their fantasies.

5

HOPE

One of the attitudes of Christianity which I still live by is its hopefulness, for the word hope has always been one of the three great words, and Christianity could never survive without it.

"Abandon hope all ye who enter here" was Dante's injunction to the damned entering hell. Now it is preached as the proper attitude for those who live. For since the great depression began (and it was no coincidence) the stylish thing has been to sneer at the doctrine of progress, and to say with increasing ponderosity and venom that there is no human progress, there is no hope. Such preachers are giving us stones to eat instead of bread. I have gone on eating the bread of hope, and propose to continue doing so.

Dr. French told me a while ago that he regarded

HOPE

hope as the one necessity for a strong ego, by which he meant a strong personality. How, then, can we hope?

In general, hope for the future is based upon knowledge of the past, a sense that the past was in some way successful, and a belief that the future will continue the promise of past experiences. A little child becomes completely depressed at each discouragement, because he has no past experience to assure him that the pain or disappointment of the present is a passing thing. Hence his utter abandonment to grief. He cannot "be a man" until he is a man with a man's memories. In the larger problems of society the experience of an individual is quite inadequate, and we must have a sense of man's historical development to see any hope for humanity.

One of the great things about the Jewish-Christian tradition is that both religions, by being rooted in the past, could help their people meet the crises of the present with hope for the future. Somehow, through all the tragedies of their history, the Jews produced prophet after prophet who, in starkest realism about the immediate catastrophes, still looked back upon God's dealing with the Jewish people to find assurance that he had a plan and a place for them in the future. The Jews were the only optimists or, if you prefer, hopeful people in antiquity: consequently they alone have a consistent history to the present. Not only did their knowledge of history give them a hope to survive, hope was the chief factor in making them survive. The Greeks, the Romans, the Syrians were without any such dimensions to their thinking or emotions, and so they crumbled before catastrophe. Only the Jews could make so extraordinary an invention as was their rabbinical tradition and literature when by all external standards they had nothing left whatever.

Nothing but hope. But that was enough. They went on telling the stories from the past of how God had called Abraham and promised to make his descendants a great people, had taken the Israelites from Egypt to the Promised Land, had saved always a few Jews from every devastation, and had built up a new future out of the remnant. So in the end a great Deliverer would come. By thus rehearsing the past they kept a vivid sense that man's problems had been solved in the ages gone, and so could be solved in the future. It is for this reason that the Jews, as they say, have stood at the graves of all their persecutors.

Christianity took over this heritage and made it available to men of all races. One of the mistakes of modern expositions of Christianity has been an overemphasis upon its novelty. The early Christians were fully aware that they had their place in the stream of the history of religion. The true message of Christianity has always been that in Christ all things have become new, indeed, but even more fundamentally that the Gospel was only the flowering of the religious dreams of the past, "the hope of the promise of God made unto our fathers." So Christians had also what they thought was a sure basis in the history of God's dealing with men in the past.

Paul, the great psychologist, saw this. The whole creation, he said, groans and travails in pain, but we are saved in hope. We do not know exactly what it is we are hoping for, he said; indeed the essence of hope is that it looks toward the unknown, the unseen, and patiently waits for it. This was a recurrent form of expression with Paul: "The patience of hope," "Rejoicing in hope, patient in tribulation," "Hopeth all things, endureth all things."

"He that ploweth shall plow in hope," said Paul, and certainly there would be little plowing without it. What is the source of hope for the farmer? Clearly it is the experience of the race with the recurrent seasons. Crops have failed often enough, and people have starved in consequence. But the percentage of returns from plowing is such that men still plow in hope. To this, a primitive man may add hope in fertility rites, or a Christian may hope in his prayers to God for rain or sun. But all hopes go back to the experience that crops do usually grow when properly planted, whether or not a hope in God is superimposed on this hope through human experience and effort.

In denouncing history as a basis for human confidence, the preachers of neo-orthodoxy, now so stylish, strike not only at the psychological roots of man, but at the heart of the Christian message. For these people are telling us that God laughs at man's efforts, that the world of time is meaningless, that man's existence is essentially a treadmill except as the eternal and timeless intervenes. Metaphysically, this may or may not be true, but it has never been the message of Christianity in general, and I refuse to allow that it is a valid statement of the faith. It may be that Christians have believed that the preservation of man from disaster has always been a special providence, a manifestation of divine intervention, that the crops, for example, are a yearly miracle of God's special favor and bounty. But still the farmer has plowed in hope because the experience of the race was that such bounties could, in general, be counted on. When it was discovered that fields with manure grew more crops than fields without it, a few may have thought that God was blessing the man for using manure, but usually no such idea entered anyone's head. Experience with manure simply aroused hope from manure. The hope, all the hope, eventually went back to human experience.

So we may hope, Christianity tells us, because of Abraham's experiences, David's experiences, the early Christians' experiences. Something has worked throughout history. It may have been God's intervention, or man's faith in God, or man's perseverance to the end, but mankind has had on the whole a successful history to this point, or we should not be here at all. The modern Roman Catholic finds great stability and hopefulness from the very age of his church. *Quod semper!* Not so old as Judaism, still it is the oldest consistent organization in our society. Its historical roots, the very sense of time, are a highly important part of Christian preaching. For only the past gives any pledge of the future.

Many Christians from the beginning, it is true, have found their hope through despairing of this world, and looking to another and better world which the faithful, at least, would enter after death. But a complete centering on the future in the next world has never been the living hope of the majority of Christians, and so has never been central in Christian life, however much it may have been the center of preaching. Christians on the whole have always been at least ambivalent about the other world, and however much they may have looked to Christ and the church to take them to heaven, have always taught that the experience of Christ should make men more just, humane, kind, in this life, and that the expansion of Christianity would mean the spreading of Christian virtues, the raising of the whole level of human existence. This has been the basis of almost all Christian missions, Catholic or Protestant. It became the essence of Christianity to the liberal Christians. Individually, Christianity gave men hope of happiness in this life, and collectively the virtues of the past would become social property as the Christian gospel was accepted and "put into practice." Even the current school of Christian preachers is still human, for if they do not talk in terms of the kingdom of God coming through world-wide evangelism, they look forward to some sort of happy resolution of human affairs in what they call the "eschaton," which is a confusing Greek term for a metaphysical approach to the same thing. Christianity, and indeed human existence, are inseparable from optimism and hope.

Our "Age of Anxiety" needs Christian hope more than any other one thing. At present, the more upsetting or discouraging a speaker or writer, the more profound he is thought to be. "Realism" is synonymous with hopelessness. We hear on every side in tones of self-assumed penetration that we have discovered science only to create a monster that will devour us. The atom bomb, communism, fascism, germ warfare, have replaced the terror of poison gas of thirty years ago. We have an obsession with despair and what we call "disillusionment." Fortunately in America it can almost be described as an occupational disease of the "upper" classes and has little affected the mass of people, who are going on very well.

Anxiety struck Germany as a result of World War I, and reduced the Germans to the point that the hopefulness of Hitler offered an irresistible relief. It struck the French with the humiliation of 1940, and where it will lead them, if not checked, does not yet appear. It came to our wealthier people with the great bubble-bursting of 1929, the depression, the terror of the New Deal, the taxes of the forties, along with the growing threat of Russia.

Now I do not take the threat of Russia lightly myself, but I belong essentially to the simple people of America, the mass of whom are more deeply intelligent

Hope

than the frightened rich and the self-conscious intelligentsia, for the masses are intelligent enough not to have lost their sense of the continuity of man. Still living largely in inherited traditions, we, the masses, take pain and pleasure as they come, and keep our balance in an ill-defined hope that if we are not making a great splash as individuals, we are bringing up our children in a society which, for all its terrible faults, is really, if very slowly, improving.

Never understanding the more extreme presentations of the doctrine of progress, as it was formulated forty years ago, we have not had to give it up for an equally silly extreme of its denial. For we know that modern science has prolonged our individual lives for decades, so that we do not have to die, broken and old, at thirty-two, or have our families swept away by the Black Death. Those of us who must see our sons go to modern wars can do so with far higher hopes of their return than did the fathers of soldiers in the wars of the past. Here modern science, in medicine and sanitation, tips the scales as against modern science in instruments of destruction. So we are not dissolving our souls in home-made pessimism.

That is, we essentially believe in ourselves and man, and, as our fathers went out into the American wilderness in the past, so we still dare to be pioneers into the future. Our fathers also believed in God, and this some of us still do, while with some of us God has become rather hazy. What founded America, however, was not so much our father's belief in God as their basic humanism, their belief in man, including themselves. That is, they were a god-fearing lot who put into their gospel as one of its major axioms: "God helps them as helps themselves."

This was not to be found in the pessimistic theory of the Calvinistic Puritan theologians, but their theology never weakened the nerve of the Puritans themselves, or their Scotch-Irish successors. The polarity of their practical Christian tradition, hope in an unpredictable but predicting God, and hope in their own efforts, has been the foundation of America. When I explain Puritan theology to my students, they always ask why it did not paralyze all human effort. Actually it stimulated men with a sense of the reality of achievement through history (history with thousands of years for its perspective), achievement brought about when industrious, just men cooperated with the great plan and Planner of the universe.

This is the heritage of the common people, the hope of our civilization.

Always, over against this mass, have been the few whose grandparents' success has indeed paralyzed their sense of the value of human effort. It is an old tradition which we have inherited from Europe and England, that the man who had an able grandfather is a cut above those who have ability themselves. The psychological effect of such an attitude upon the grandchildren may be devastating. From youth, such grandchildren are given the psychological attitude of old age. For the man who has worked hard wants as

Hope

he gets older to die with the fruit of his achievements, whether money or scholarship or his standing as a doctor. The tax collector who will take away the old man's farm or money, the young scholar who demonstrates the old scholar's inadequacy, the young doctor who proves to be a better doctor with the new methods, these are all threats to the old man who cannot begin again, and who wants the security of his old ways and conquests.

It is a bad thing when young people inherit such an attitude toward rival accomplishment, when they hope for security also in the achievements of their grandfathers. The young who with inherited money or social prestige have inherited as well a terror of the novel, so that they cling to the old, these are pitiable in a way we common people are not. And yet it is these old-spirited youngsters who are apt to be the spokesmen and guides of the day, men whose chief aim is to hold the old line, their grandfathers' line.

It is these who express their terror at our rapidly changing civilization in terms of the bogies of the day, whatever they may be. The Christian churches have had to adjust to such people for centuries, to their nostalgia for the recent past, their constant reiteration that the younger generations have no such stuff as the old. Too often the churches have played up to these people because they were the ones with money to paint the church and to pay the minister. As a result the churches have seemed often the instruments of the conservative classes, the opiate of the lower classes to keep them in their place. It is for this reason that the apostles of doom, of human helplessness, are now so widely heard. The appalling new problems which the shrinking of the world, the dependence of each part of the world on all other parts, has brought, have staggered these inelastic people, and made them turn back to all sorts of new-old formulations in which there seemed to be some security.

It is natural that this sort of mentality should have rejected the doctrine of progress. Progress has actually been coming too fast for them. That citizens of the United States should pay taxes to feed Arabs or build roads in Turkey, or to give old-age security to employees, this is indeed hard for such people to take. Threatened by taxes, by the emergence of the masses from slavery which the history of trade unionism represents, by a thousand demands for recognition from the common people, the conservative mind must indeed reject all conceptions of progress. Progress has become to conservatives an abstraction which is like what, in its human form, they call a "bounder," and they condemn the one as emotionally as they do the other.

Now I have no brief for the shallow optimism common a generation ago among the scientists and their popularizers. When I was a student at Oxford thirty years ago, I remember hearing one of its great physicists, a Nobel Prize winner, say that science had proved there was no God because science had climbed up into the driving compartment of the universe, and had encountered no opposition when it took over the throttle and began running things itself. It is certainly a relief not to hear that sort of nonsense any more. The very loss of it, however, means the return of man to a sense of his insignificance in the universe—a new and better way of expressing what our fathers meant when they said that man is a worm in God's sight. The return to the idea in its better expression is itself a splendid example of progress. For the goal of human effort is that man learn his possibilities and limitations, and come to the best life possible in the universe, whatever the best may prove to be. It seems to me that in keeping that old scientist's discoveries, and in rejecting his arrogance, we have made real progress toward that goal.

For the advances of science of the last generation have taught man not that he knows, but that the universe, and man himself, is a great mystery which we do not remotely understand. This is extremely disquieting to those who by their social security and creeds have lived in a closed and manageable world. It is not disquieting at all to us common men, who have never lived in anything but a mysterious universe. The great unwritten tradition which has given common men their courage in the face of personal frustrations is to accept the mystery as mystery, to find out as well as they could what would help them (like manure on their fields, or justice in society), and to carry on. We are the great mass of humanity who, in Paul's words, "against hope have believed in hope."

There is no reason why we should abandon that tradition. Thus far the universe, or, if you prefer, God, has worked with man in his struggle to find himself. Knowledge of human history, Christianity at its best teaches us, is the great source, the only source, of hope for man. New revelations, or, if you will, discoveries, have steadily come to man as he needed them and arduously sought them. We may live in an indifferent world, theoretically, but man's very survival shows that we do not live in a hostile universe, and I see no reason or ground to insist that the universe is even indifferent. To make a dogma of the universe's indifference goes as far beyond our knowledge as to assert that it was made and is ruled by a Spirit benevolently interested especially in man. The one is as much a projection of foolish despair as the other is of smugness. We do not know enough about the universe to make any such generalizations either objective or meaningful.

This we do know, that the experience of man through the last million years, which is what we must go on, is that the universe cooperates at least to the extent that it has allowed man to come into existence, to survive, and to develop in a marvelous way. Accordingly, even if we ourselves as personalities are quite ephemeral, and we do not look to a future life for ourselves, we may still face the world with the basic confidence of Christians and Jews because of the experiences of our fathers. We may hope in the God, or nature, of the universe who, we still hope, will yet save us as our fathers were saved.

So one basis of hope is in the very character of the

Hope

universe itself. The other ground of hope is in ourselves.

One hopeless fellow has recently proved the degeneration of man by the increasing size of our wars! That is a common line of attack. As though David or Alexander or Hannibal or Cato or Julius Caesar or Frederick the Great or Louis XIV or Napoleon or Kaiser Wilhelm stopped their wars where they did for any reason but that they could go no farther with the weapons they had, and with their means of locomotion and of getting supplies! The least imperialistic people in all history were the first to use the atomic bomb—for the simple reason that they had it first. The history of man can indeed be written in terms of his increasing skill in warfare and destruction. But this does not mean that primitive man was a more kindly creature than we are. When the noble Romans took a city, such as Carthage, they killed or enslaved all its inhabitants and erased the city itself until they could run a plow over its former site. Even the atom bomb was not so thorough. That the Romans could not destroy so quickly as we can is no sign of greater humanity on the part of the Romans.

The point is that if history can be written in terms of man's increasing power to destroy his fellows, it can also be written in terms of his increasing respect for his fellows, of his growing skill in feeding the hungry, in healing the sick, in controlling natural disasters, and in getting himself out of bad situations. It has some-

Toward a Mature Faith

times taken man centuries to solve his difficulties, but when he became aware of them he has always found a way out.

We are now faced with increasing complexity in life. The one world is a far more complicated machine to learn to run than the city of Athens. The Athenians had only temporary success in solving their problems in the way they wanted, that is by humiliating and getting tribute from all their neighboring city states. If like the Athenians we also take the wrong way, we shall likewise fail to achieve the goal.

This does not mean that all human effort is constructive, or all equally to be praised. We see that those who have lived by justice and cooperation have continued, whether as nations or as a people, while the nations which have lived on arrogance and force have not. The old belief that humanity survives better through justice and kindness than through violence and greed has every right to appeal to the history of imperial nations. Modern writers on the theory of history who have wanted to make everything cyclic and futile have missed the survival value of the basic virtues as revealed in history. If they have survival value they must also in some way accord with the nature of things. This has been the reasoning of many in the past, and the reasoning seems to me flawless. And so they are the basis of hope.

There is a right way, and, by indefinite blundering man will find it. That is not promise of immediate perfection. It may take us centuries or millennia to find the solutions. But sooner or later there is every hope that mankind will find them.

Here our oldest tradition, our religious tradition, can help us more than anything else, for it can best of all give us a sense of the millennia of human effort, effort toward the right way, and hence of hope for the struggle in the millennia ahead. You and I will die with the problems in which we are most deeply concerned unsolved, and so will our great-grandchildren. Their descendants may not be the ones to survive by solving these problems. But in a world that is as much for man as a whole as it is against him, at least, and in view of man's proved ability to muddle through in the long run, there is no reason why we may not live with the light of hope within us and before us.

6

LOVE

An interesting thing about the Judaeo-Christian tradition is that many of its deepest sayings, those of eternal and changeless value, are put in the form of commands to do the impossible. "Thou shalt love thy neighbor as thyself." Jesus selected this from Leviticus to make it one of his two basic commands. And he took the rabbinical command to do nothing to others which we would not like them to do to us, a difficult enough command, but one which can be applied. He took this and put it in the positive form, that we should do to our associates what we should like them to do to us. In this form it is impractical because we are never in a position to do everything to others which we should like to have done to ourselves. It makes us always guilty.

Self-love is man's deepest instinct. What we used to call the instinct of self-preservation, all that we put

LOVE

into the word ambition, in its best as well as its worse senses, the craving for education, for self-expression, for self-fulfillment, even religious self-fulfillment, these are all aspects of self-love. A woman loves her self and her husband (her other self), as well as her children, and in trying to make the children conform to her best ideals of truth, reliability, courtesy, intelligence, she is in the children fulfilling her own ideals. When they fail, she is as humiliated as though she had failed herself. Our craving to dress properly and becomingly, if not elegantly, to make a place for ourselves in one way or another in society, to be loved deeply by a husband or wife, all of these are manifestations of self-love. Even the mystic who loses himself in the being of God finds himself, the greatest of all discoveries, in losing himself.

The commandment then comes that we love in this way, just as we do ourselves, not our special friend, or husband, or children, but our neighbor—that is, all fellow human beings. The reference is not to those occasional fits of heroism by which a man will rush into a burning house and give his life trying to save a neighbor, or will drown with a perfect stranger whom he sees sinking in the water. If that were so, the professional firemen, policemen, and life-guards on the beach would be the great examples of Christian love, rivaled only by the spirit of love in the Army and Navy! Clearly, that is not what the command refers to. Much more it refers to our life in ordinary society in normal conditions, and here the command becomes fantastic. I may respect my neighbors as human beings, fight for their rights, help them in trouble, even enjoy the society of some of them. But love them, each of them, all of them, with the same elaborate and complicated devotion with which I maintain my own coherence in self-regard and self-love? Hardly.

Similarly, I can respond to the Golden Rule by treating my neighbor with such respect and justice and kindness as I would expect from him. But to do everything to everyone which it would *please* me to have done to me, that is another matter. I can do to others all that I have any reason or hope to expect from them. But to do everything I should *like* done to me? That suggestion produces only preposterous confusion in me.

Christianity has for the most part carried such commands as supercargo in its ethical codes. In their more extreme, that is, in their literal, implications they have been interpreted as commands only for the "perfect," a term taken from Jesus' preface to one of his most difficult commands, "If thou wilt become perfect." But these statements have never ceased to haunt men, to check their smugness, to make them dissatisfied with their more reasonable and possible adjustments and patterns of living. What we might have been content with doing and feeling in society has always turned out to be not enough. These commands for centuries have spurred men to deeper insights, more adequate ideas of the scope of justice and social cooperation. They have created in us the unrest without which develop-

LOVE

ment, not to say progress, in social life is impossible. In their very impossibility of fulfillment lies their power, and their value.

They are far from having outlived their usefulness, and by their very form of expression are easily adaptable to modern thinking. For both commands use the individual's self-love, desire for place and recognition in, and benefit from, society, as the criterion for one's duties in society. This is often forgotten in modern exposition, which takes from them their genuine, if paradoxical, realism.

It has been the fashion lately to say in Christian circles that the great contribution of Christianity was that it used the Greek word *agapē* instead of *eros* for love—the love of God and the love of man for man. This new Christian love, it is taught, is not a love which desires self-gratification, but one which seeks only to benefit others, is self-abandonment. That no such difference inheres in the two Greek words will not interest the general reader, but is well known to all students of Greek. In fact the distinction must seem a barbarism to any classicist.

The fact is that this very command of Jesus is a quotation from the Old Testament, and accordingly is not a Christian innovation. The command is, however, a deep part of Christian tradition and its interpretation as love which disregards self-interest completely robs it of its value. It, and the Golden Rule, are of abiding pertinence in modern thought precisely because they do no such thing. Self-love as the criterion of love for one's neighbor in no sense disregards or destroys the fact of self-love. And that we should treat our neighbors as we should like to be treated still recognizes man's passion to be treated properly himself. To disregard this aspect of man is to reduce the whole to a sentimentality repugnant to contemporary thinking. The sentimentality is in the recent interpretations, not in the words themselves.

For actually in the words is epitomized one of the most important contributions of Christianity, its recognition of the individual as a highly important form of existence, coupled with the obligation to respect the feelings and rights of other individuals. The teaching of Christianity by no means submerges the individual in social obligations, even though it recognizes that in the perfect society each individual would be aware that he is only one among many. It is almost Freudian to be told that the libido (Freud's term for the basic love instinct and so an accurate translation of *agapē*) which rules our lives as individuals must expand to be the ruling principle in our relation to others. Freudian, yes, but far beyond Freud, whose preoccupation with the libido in the individual made Freudianism so individualistic that it has seemed a disruptive influence in constructing a social philosophy. The important emphasis of the Christian tradition upon both the value of the individual and of social cooperation and obligation, however much the two may sometimes seem to clash, is what I want to discuss in this chapter.

Love

The Individual

Our modern sense of the value of a human individual is largely an inheritance from the Christian tradition. Democracy is inconceivable without it; that is, the conception that the opinion of every man living in a country is of equal value with that of everyone else, high or low, rich or poor, intelligent or stupid, informed or uninformed. No myth, incidentally, could be more amazingly bizarre. But it works better than any social myth known to history. It works for the good of the individuals and of society as a whole. Over and over, in the slow development of the basic laws of individual rights summarized in the Bill of Rights, people have appealed to the Christian picture of man made in the image of God, of every person appearing before the final judgment as an individual, of Christ dying for individual salvation, of his interest in the "least of these."

Christianity emerged in a society where slavery was a matter of course, and the humble first Christians had no thought of abolishing it. Hence in the great debate within the churches before the Civil War the Southern preachers, who favored slavery, had all the proof texts. But the implications of the Bible so enhanced the dignity of the individual, whether Jew or Greek, bond or free, that the Southerners themselves would now almost unanimously admit that in this debate the Northern preachers were closer to the real spirit of Christianity. The same is true of the growing recognition of the human rights of factory workers in the North, in the course of which we have corrected conditions which Southerners are quite right in saying were at least as bad as the slavery of the South. Our armies use the term "expendables," but can use it with no such freedom as the Russians and Chinese, precisely because of the Christian tradition of the value of the individual person. Even the Germans thought our soldiers cowards, no fighters, because of the care we took to put our men into no avoidable jeopardy.

Race distinction and snobbery, all sorts of special privilege, persist from the primordial social structures, but we increasingly recognize that they are contrary to the Christian spirit. In the broadening of our concern for people of all classes, the right of every man to his opinions and his basic human dignity, we witness the Christian heritage still slowly winning over the primordial. When it comes to extending this right to the unborn, so that even birth control is opposed on the Christian ground of the sanctity of the individual, I myself feel that we are taking a good idea to absurdity. But infanticide is out. Once he is born, the baby has his inalienable rights. Even idiots and the insane must be given kindly, ultimately Christian, treatment. Individuals must be given not only the right to live, but to develop their human dignity by universal education. It is a Christian expansion when we increasingly feel that even the most erudite and costly forms of education must be available for individuals of every class who are competent to receive them.

LOVE

I would not rule Judaism out from this, for a large part of our Bible is the Jews' as well, and the host of great rabbis in Jewish history who came from the humblest families is part of the glory of Jewish tradition. In our own day, certainly, the Jewish names in the list of any sort of fund for public mercy often shame the Christians by their disproportion in number and generosity. Still, early Judaism is part of the Christian tradition and in modern history Judaism has been an active influence for too short a time for it to have made basic contributions anew to our social traditions. How far Jesus was only formulating Jewish ideas we need not debate. The fact is that the ideas were carried out into gentile civilizations by the Church in the name of Jesus, and his expressions of them are still the classical ones.

For on the basis of the Old Testament conception that man is made in the image of God, from which he derives his inherent dignity as an individual, Jesus went beyond the Old Testament in his amazing statements. Jeremiah had insisted that God is interested in the individual to the point that "the soul that sinneth, *it* shall die" rather than that God was, like the pagan gods, the sort which sent pestilence and devastation to whole societies because of some offensive person or group of persons in the land. And such Psalms as the Twenty-Third testify to God's interest in the (righteous) individual. But nothing in the Old Testament goes so far as the parable of the Good Samaritan, where the human equality of even aliens is stressed; or the Good Shepherd who leaves his ninety-nine sheep to search for the wandering hundredth, and brings it back on his shoulders; or the extraordinary statement which Jesus says he will make at the Last Judgment, "Inasmuch as you did it unto the least of these you did it unto me," by which it is taught that in dealing with even beggars and outcasts, we are dealing with God himself. The idea is carried to the fantastic lengths of God counting the hairs of our head, and having individual respect and concern for birds and flowers of the field. These overstatements have always been taken for what they really are, literary devices for emphasizing the value of the human individual as such.

This was the first step in Christianity toward creating self-respect in man, only another term for the self-love which must underlie our love of others. It was stated in the fanciful, mythical, form which the masses could understand. What it did was to make the slave, the great mass of the hopeless in the ancient world, have hope. For the first time it offered them a way of seeing themselves as respectable, important, dignified parts, however small, in the universe. The best the pagan world had to offer was a philosophy of resignation and acceptance of life's tragedies and joys alike, or an esoteric mysticism of escape and union with the One. Both were based upon the individual's recognition of his unimportance as a human being, and both were as remote from the life of the ordinary man then as now. Both made man psychologically an orphan, a rejected child, rejected by the universe as much as by society. Here could be no self-respect or love, and accordingly

LOVE

no respect or love of others. Where there was no sense of one's own dignity, the sport of human torture in the arena was inevitable.

The statements of Jesus, while never forgotten, were too stark, too basic, to be adequate. Always they have acted as a living yeast in the theological dough which Christianity quickly baked to feed its followers. One such saying, "It is more blessed to give than receive," even crept into Paul's writing, much as he scorned the tradition of Jesus' form of teaching in general. Christian theology, as it began in Paul and the author of the Gospel of John, accepted the pagan notion of the inherent state of rejection of the individual in his natural form of existence. Paul had no beggar, like Lazarus, who went to heaven just because society had put him in the gutter while he was alive.

Paul and John, however, while they rejected the dignity of human nature as such, went much more deeply into the psychological problems of man's experiences with himself. They were aware that man does not accept himself, that he is beaten down by inner condemnations of his natural instincts, that there are terrible tensions between what Paul called the desires of his members, and his idealism, or sense of right. His discussion of this in the seventh chapter of Romans is one of the most amazing premonitions of later Freudianism.

For, as I explained more briefly before, Freud too divided the psyche into parts, or saw three principles or centers at work in it. The one, called the "id," is the drive to gratify the desires of the body, but goes beyond that into what is ordinarily called self-assertion, the establishment of the individual over against society, God, or fate. It gives us that aggressiveness which Freud rightly saw is so deeply important a part of our life pattern. Over against this is a second center, which Freud called the "ego ideal" or "superego." It begins with the control exercised over us in infancy by our parents. This control we transfer within ourselves, until we say "No, no!" "Naughty, naughty!" to ourselves. It grows beyond this, however, and becomes the whole pattern of society to which we feel we must conform. Indeed we take society within us, and become Americans, or Zulus, or members of a class, by becoming so in our very inner structure. If our environment includes God, or the gods, as has been the case for the vast majority of the human race, the compulsion to comply with the divine will has likewise been a part of man's superego. Even if we do not use such a word as God, still we have our ideals to which we feel obliged to conform. All of these function as a unit to compel us to check the impulses of the id; that is, they are what we call ordinarily our conscience. They also function as a positive force in our ideals. The idealistic, positive, function of this part of us Freud did not, in my opinion, sufficiently stress. The neurotics of Vienna were not, presumably, idealists. But in a psychology of religion this part of the superego's work becomes highly important.

Between these two is a third principle of Freud,

LOVE

one which he called the "ego." The function of the ego is to pull together the discordant tendencies of the id and superego, and so give us unity, self-confidence, poise within ourselves. The ego also has the work of aligning us with "reality," the facts of life, and seems to be the seat of what little reasoning power we have in contrast to the rationalizations of our bodily desires or our ideals.

These three appear vividly in this extraordinary passage of Paul,[1] and we shall return to them in the following chapters. Here we need note only that Paul describes how what he calls "I," the Freudian ego, was helplessly pulled back and forth between the demands of his sense of right and the compulsions of his "members," his bodily desires. My ego, my "I," sees the better (that is, what is presented to him by the superego) and passionately desires it, says Paul. But "I" do the worse. Wretched man that "I" am, exclaimed Paul's ego, caught between the two. How can there be self-love when one sees oneself constantly humiliated and vanquished in an inner struggle? Of course, Paul concluded, God has rejected us as ignominious failures. We still feel the rejection today as our own superegos loathe our actual life patterns.

Paul's preaching and writing only brought this struggle, and its constant failure, out of the unconscious. It was everywhere in man, and still is everywhere, though some can repress it more successfully than others. But a self-love won through repression is an artificial tour de force, and as we steel ourselves to ig-

[1] Romans 7:19, 24.

nore our own moral failures, we harden ourselves in relation to others. The early theologians, profound psychologists, recognized that the only way of safety was to face our inner turmoil, and so to rebuild ourselves, strengthen our superegos to such a point, that we can live without what Paul called inner "condemnation," and feel ourselves acceptable to ourselves because we have become acceptable to God.

This experience he called dying and rising with Christ as a new creature; the Fourth Gospel called it being "born again." Both are powerful figures, with great psychological implications.

Now it is not the question here whether you and I believe that God so loved the world that he sent his only Son that whosoever would accept him would not perish but come into the new and true form of living. The point is that the early Christians found in this formula the solution of their problem. They went out into the Roman world with that as their message, and convinced a sufficient part of the Roman world that this method really did work. The result was that the Roman world became the Christian world. They went with this message to the outcasts of society, and the combination of the charm of Jesus' fancy, the inspiration of his paradoxes, along with the psychological insight of the theologians, brought them for the first time inner healing and basic self-love. Though the values achieved by the convulsive experience preached by Paul and later Protestant evangelists were made more humanly and generally available by the Church in ritual and sacrament, still the effect was to give man at last a sense of being accepted in the world, a child of love surrounded by love, and so ready to show love to others.

Thus, each in his own way, Jesus and the Christian theologians taught man to value every individual as a child of God. Whether we accept Jesus' fancies in literal form, or Christian theology, is perhaps important. But it is much more important that we learn from them that man must come into self-acceptance, acceptance not as a rejected worm, but as a being, however small and apparently insignificant, with a place in the universe and in human history. This place we still can describe only in terms of fancies, yet it is a place, so that through a sense of belonging we can face the problems of life, even the most terrible problems of all, those within our own souls.

The churches through the past have seemed often to forget this message of the value of the individual, especially our obligation to treat everyone with the consideration we desire for ourselves, as for centuries they supported aristocracy and social privilege, and taught the lower classes the duty of subservience. In modern centuries, men like Locke, Rousseau, Voltaire, John Adams, Comte, and Marx felt themselves outside the Christian tradition in supporting popular rights. They were certainly outside general Christian practice. But the churches continued to pay lip service to the teachings of Jesus; and the monastic orders, conspicuously the early Franciscans, often put them into extraordinary practical reality. The churches indeed never ceased to emphasize the dignity of all men before God (that is, men's essential if not social value), and in looking for the salvation of the poor along with the rich, in exalting to sainthood hundreds of the lowliest men and women, they kept before men the idea of a cosmic democracy which had sooner or later to register in human relations.

I have asked friends who do not call themselves Christians what, in their opinion, is the greatest permanent contribution of Christianity. Most commonly they have said that it was the Christian tradition of the value of the individual. It is not by chance that the totalitarian states, and such philosophies as those of Nietzsche by which those states were largely influenced, denounced Christianity most of all for its emphasis upon the individual and his importance. From a purely pragmatic point of view, we cannot treat lightly the Christian doctrine, even though we may prefer it as Jesus expressed it rather than as it appeared in the theology of Paul.

Social

The value of the individual, his self-love in the Christian sense, which is his craving to develop his powers whether in relation to this world or the next, has meant both for Jesus and his theological followers that we must also recognize the dignity of others. If Jesus could take self-love for granted, the emphasis of his command was upon the necessity of expanding this self-love to one's neighbors. He was never so unrealistic as to forget this double obligation. True, giving a cup of cold water to the thirsty, Jesus assured us, would be considered of great importance at the Last Judgment in determining whether a person went to heaven or hell, so that there was no lack of appeal to self-love in recommending that one give the cup of water. But the point was that Jesus was teaching men that the way to the highest achievements for oneself is not through direct concern for oneself but for those who need help.

This is one of the paradoxes of human life. Self-development, like happiness, is rarely achieved by direct approach. No one is less happy than the man trying to make himself so. Only as we find something so absorbing that we forget whether we are happy or not can we hope to look back upon a day or a period of life and call it happy. A man looking for amusement, seeking thrills, is a man trying to escape inner unhappiness, whether of emptiness or guilt. Escape through alcohol or drugs is little less futile as a road to happiness than escape through thrills or amusement. Real happiness comes only to those who have become so interested in some forms or form of creative activity that they forget to ask themselves whether they are happy or not.

It is so with self-development or self-love. The conscious attempt at its achievement is futile. A student who works at chemistry or literature to get recognition in high grades, or, later, in appointments on faculties, may get the grades or the appointments, or may win great distinction as a learned man; but his fellows call him a grind, an academic climber, and see that as a person he is quite hollow. The person who has "lost himself" in his interest in painting, in the laboratory, in creative scholarship of any kind, who studies because the problems fascinate him so that he must understand and think them through, does not impress us as a grind at all, but as one whose life is truly rich. "If I could only get really interested in something in the way Jack loves medicine!" is the most pathetic remark I hear from young people. Such people are tragic because they are so engrossed in self-love that they have lost the power of self-development. For the paradox of Jesus is still completely true, that only the one who loses himself can find himself.

This, Jesus profoundly indicated, is true also in social relationships. He told us that when we give a dinner party we are to select our guests not on the basis of immediate self-love—that is, invite those who will return the invitation, or whom it will flatter our vanity to have as acquaintances—but among those who need a dinner. As usual, Jesus made his point by overstating it. But we know very well what he meant. He despised the social climber, the man who approached social relations with self-love, self-advantage, as his guiding principle. Nothing but personal hollowness (we see it in other persons) can result from snobbery. The only way to self-development through social relations is to forget oneself, at least in the conscious mind, and to become genuinely interested in other people.

Love

I remember being looked over by a wise old professor at Yale for my first appointment. I had never taught, and he was trying to make up his mind whether this young Ph.D. would also make a teacher. He did not ask me if I were a fluent speaker, or organized my thinking clearly. He simply read my dissertation, and then asked, "Do you like boys?" Scholarly qualifications were essential, yes. But they were of no use for the elementary teaching then in question unless I was going to enjoy trying to develop immature minds and personalities. All successful living is thus an expansion of one's self-love to the place that, in Freudian terms, we "identify" ourselves with others. When the struggling mediocre student begins, even at what would be a low level for a bright boy, to grasp a subject; when the boy of brilliant mentality masters and begins to think independently and creatively, so that he nettles the professor by asking questions which throw the professor off base; this is real "finding himself" for the professor who has properly identified himself with his students. Their development has become his development, and such a teacher seems to his students a rich, fully developed personality.

The same holds true in all other relations. A man is not truly married who does not find in his wife his "better half." She is not truly a mother who does not find in her children's satisfaction and growth the most important part of her own growth, to the point that she has largely forgotten the problem of her own growth. The woman who has personal ambitions, social, financial or other, so that her children and household duties are a frustration to her, is indeed disloyal in her heart, one who seeks satisfaction for herself outside the family. It is not that a woman should have no outside contacts or interests. Many women who are magnificent mothers and wives have regular appointments outside the home. But when outside appointments, or the desire for them, interfere with her wholeheartedly identifying herself with her husband and children, not only will her family suffer, her own ego will go sour.

In such identification there is danger, great danger, for herself and children alike. When her devotion to husband and children leads to such remarks as "I work for you day and night, I go nowhere, I wear wretched old clothes, and look at your ingratitude!" they owe her no gratitude at all, for if she wants gratitude, adulation, she has not really "lost herself," but has been using them for her own ends. However devoted she may appear to her neighbors, she will be despised at home, or rather regarded with a bewildering conflict of love and hate which will lead to neuroses in all concerned. There is no substitute for genuineness, no possibility of deception in such matters. If our self-love is so strong that identification with others can be only simulated, we may convince our conscious minds that we are sincere, even appear to be so to outsiders, but the conflicts of our inner tensions will tear us. Our children, without analysis, will know perfectly well that we are as much against them as with

LOVE

them, and will react accordingly. Claims for gratitude, expressed or implicit, only antagonize and repel.

Unfortunately some of us are clever, and actually do deceive our children, to the point that we make them live our lives rather than their own. We all have known "mother's boys," unable to marry, or, if they do marry, still identifying with the mother rather than with the wife. Their mothers usually (not always) seem at first meeting to be very attractive. In a large number of cases, these women were early widowed, and the sensitive boy identified himself with the grief-stricken mother rather than she with him. Thereafter, the more she seemed to devote herself to the boy, the more she was actually enslaving him to herself. Self-love had dominated, to the pathetic distorting of the boy, and to the making of herself into what is to me always a repellent creature, one who could not love even her son "as herself." Had she gone out and had a career in which she became deeply interested, really lost herself in something else, she could have freed the boy of what became to him a crushing burden.

Similarly a father who must control and direct a son, so that the son completes the father's life rather than his own, has really not followed Jesus' most profound advice. I remember a father who came to see me. He was a fabulously wealthy man who had built up a great business by his own unusually creative initiative. His son was studying with me, and had become deeply interested in Greek traditions, especially in Greek philosophy, and was considering going into such study for his life work. The father, in striped trousers and derby hat, suddenly burst into my office and laid down the law to me, an astonished and then young teacher. There was to be no monkey business, he said. His boy was to carry on the great industry; his notion of becoming a professor was intolerable; and I was to talk to the boy thereafter with this sense of his future clearly in mind. Then he walked out.

The boy was in a terrible quandary, since for many years he had been confronted with this attitude that he must live his father's life. That was in his Sophomore year. He had not solved his problem by Senior year, and came to talk with me. He wanted to go abroad and study classics further. In the course of long conversations I agreed with him that he should take the extra time for study, but that he should watch himself, and come to a decision that he felt was his own rather than his father's. Actually, to succeed his father in the business would open up a very large and important life for him. If, as he really concentrated in graduate study, he found that this was to be his absorbing interest, and that he had a real sense of mastery in it, he would himself decide to go on in scholarship regardless of his father. But if he saw that he was going to be only a second-rate scholar, who through life would be looking over his shoulder at the opportunity he had turned down, he would probably feel that he had better go into the business now, and be happy about it. After a year at Cambridge University he came to me and said

LOVE

he had decided to go into his father's business, and he has had a very happy life in it. But the father I have never ceased to regard as a man twisted and narrowed by self-love, even though his advice for the boy was very good.

Many talks I have had with boys who were forced by parents into law or medicine or whatever, when the parents' supposed projection into the boys had been only attempts at absorbing the boys into themselves. Jesus was right when he said that we should love others, even our children, *as* ourselves, not *for* ourselves.

Obviously this applies to love between man and wife. Those are the happy ones in such a relation who love each other as they do themselves, that is who find their own personalities completed in the personality of the other, not in trying, by domination, to absorb the other into themselves. Dominance can be met only by submission and deterioration, or by rebellion. For a woman to love her husband as a mate is one thing. For her to submit to him as a master is another. The first can be done with self-love which grows in love of the other; the second can be done only with self-despising. Each must *freely give* his life for the other, and so find his life. There is great love and achievement in giving oneself, but only destruction in being robbed of oneself, or in robbing another of himself. All of this will, of course, be quite unconscious and uncalculated. True achievement is to be found only in spontaneously following Jesus' formula, loving the other as oneself.

Toward a Mature Faith

In social relations outside the family, the basic meaning of the formula is still entirely true. In recent Christian teaching it has been distorted as the extolling of "self-sacrifice." I have recently read a German study in which the key word was *Selbstpreisgabe*, self-abandonment, which was presented as the ideal. The modern man is usually, and rightly, repelled by such unreal sentimentality. Self-sacrifice for its own sake means a sort of perversion, a masochism, which indeed ends in self-destruction. The person who does something for me because he likes me and enjoys doing it does something I can accept and love him for doing. The person who does something for me "in a spirit of self-sacrifice" nauseates me. An Albert Schweitzer who feels intolerable guilt at the way the white man has degraded the black, and who simply cannot be happy in a civilization fatted by colonial spoils (as was Europe when Schweitzer went to Africa before the First World War), would be the first to agree that he hates the approach of self-sacrifice. The Negroes in Africa had become part of his own personality, and in going to them he was only expanding his self-love. To try to ignore their suffering would have created intolerable suffering within himself, because they had become part of himself. He went to Africa not to crucify himself, not to sacrifice himself, but, since he had come to include the Africans within himself, to save himself by helping them.

Clifford Beers, the lifelong worker for reform in

psychiatric institutions and one of the great constructive social workers in American history, was a manic-depressive who periodically had to be put into an institution. Destructive self-love would have led him, like most of us, to try to escape all memory of those ghastly experiences in the intervals. His constructive career was possible because he accepted the institutions, and even more his fellow-sufferers in them, as part of himself, and loved them as himself. Alcoholics Anonymous has no use for social reformers who want to make drunkards into puritans like themselves; that is, who are aggrandizing themselves in their efforts. It succeeds because its members are all alcoholics who find their best escape from their own weakness by identifying themselves with other alcoholics, and actively trying to help the others. They strengthen themselves as they strengthen others, and can do so not by condescending to the unfortunates beneath them, but by seeing the other drunkards as their alter egos.

Constructive self-love must always begin by a recognition that one's neighbor is really a part of oneself. "We are not our own." We are the product of society, of history. It means a great deal to me that I live in a house in part two centuries old. The screams of travail, the agony of death, the funerals, the weddings, the generations of young children, the joys of hundreds of birthdays and Christmases, tragedy, drunkenness, happy passion and illicit love—all these, I know, have gone on in this house. Now in living in it I live in the rich echoes of all that life. It is my own, and I am only adding one more life pattern to its continuity.

We all of us live in this way, even in a prefabricated house in a new suburb. For we have the religion, the literature, the ethical traditions, the social and political structures which our fathers collectively have worked out in agony and triumph. "We are not our own." Society may ask us dramatically to give it our lives in war; Jesus was right when he said that the demand for our lives is no less in peace. "Isolationism" (I was an isolationist in the thirties and until Pearl Harbor) broke down when we were forced to take our place as the leaders of the world, with world responsibility. It will take us long as a people to become aware of those responsibilities, and to accept them. It will be possible only as we expand our self-love to see that our "self" includes the nations of the world, since we are part of them, and they of us. We can love our neighbors as ourselves only when we see that our neighbors are really part of ourselves, that our prosperity, happiness, security, are inseparable from theirs.

Individual "isolationism" is similarly unrealistic. "We are not our own," which I repeatedly quote, is one of the great messages of the Bible, and is just as true whether we consider that the large unit to which we belong is God or human society. We must outgrow, whether in religious or social terms, the famous old prayer:

Love

God bless me and my wife,
My son John and his wife,
Us four and no more;
Glory to God for evermore.

The man who made this prayer had at least expanded his self to include three others, which is more than most of us have done. Jesus commanded us to regard the hated alien, the Samaritan, as part of ourselves, as "belonging." This is the only unsentimental approach to the problem of relations with one's neighbor. Never forgetting the claim and right of the individual, the individual recognizes himself for what he is, a part of society, and knows that he is complete only as he functions with other members as being essentially parts of himself. He can say as truly as Jesus, "Inasmuch as ye did it unto the least of these, ye did it unto me," if he has the awareness which Jesus had of the essential unity of the human race. For what helps anyone in society, here or in Tunis, helps me. "Thou shalt love thy neighbor as thyself," because he is a part of thyself.

So in presenting the value of the individual, alongside the obligation of the individual to society, Christianity has stressed an eternal problem, accentuated a perennial and universal inner tension. There is no pat resolution of this tension. Every generation, every individual must work it out afresh. But the world can ill afford to forget the Christian stressing of the problem, and its leaving the problem open. I myself believe that one of the great causes for the development of Western civilization has been the fact that Christianity throughout the centuries has increased this tension by never allowing the individual either to be lost in society, or to forget his social responsibilities.

7

SALVATION

One of the deepest teachings of Christianity has been its doctrine of salvation. This is based upon the belief that the human animal *au naturel* is a pretty poor thing, and that unless something is done, one can expect little virtue from him. Whether our perversity is thought to have arisen out of a guilt we have inherited from Adam, or is considered a matter of each man's natural weakness, according to Christian teaching we are all in a bad way, and there is no health in us.

Christianity, however, has always gone on to say that something can be, has been, done about it. There is "grace" which Christ released for us by dying on the cross and rising from the dead. When this grace comes to us, it not only washes away the old guilt, but makes us new creatures, changes our characters. Only the most extreme Christians have taught that after this happens man does not sin any more. On the contrary the Catholic churches suppose that even the most saintly should get absolution right up to death, and the grace given in Communion. But all branches of Christianity have insisted that by this grace men are definitely improved during their lifetime over what they would be without it.

This is the old doctrine, and let us be fair about it. If we do not believe in the grace of Christ and his salvation as things with historical and metaphysical existence, we cannot deny that millions through the ages have been "saved"—that is, enormously improved—by believing just that about Christ, and by "accepting" his grace. To doubt this is not scientific reserve, but the capital crime of the scientific age, prejudiced refusal to believe a fact.

I shall discuss the conception from the more typically Protestant point of view, that we can get grace from God directly, without sacramental help, although it is an idea, I hasten to add, which is by no means limited to the Protestants. That is of no importance to us here. Our concern is with the Christian doctrine that man is naturally an inner mess, which registers in outer acts of sin, but that there is help available from God to change him. This conception, I believe, still has profound value, even though many modern minds would prefer terms other than the traditional ones to describe it.

The conception of the inferiority and guilt of man is actually as prevalent now as it has ever been. Yet it

Salvation

has never been universal. William James divided those who had it from those who did not as the basic distinction in his *Varieties of Religious Experience*. Those who felt guilty and in need of help he called sick souls, those who did not he called healthy minded. The materials he quoted in his brilliant description of each type certainly show a contrast, but I doubt if the contrast is one of illness and health.

Euphoria, bland happiness, can be as pathological as a sense of guilt, and the manic stage is quite as much one of illness as is depression. Sensitivity to one's defects and failures is a normal and, within limits, healthy sign, and insensitivity in such matters by no means in itself indicates psychological balance. The contrast between those who feel guilty and those who do not, like that between the sick and the well, actually goes back to Jesus himself, who said that those who are whole do not need a physician, unlike those who are ill, and that it was these he hoped to heal. But the remark was obviously one of Jesus' bitter sarcasms. He considered the "whole" ones, the self-satisfied, to be really incurably ill by their not recognizing their inadequacy. Spiritual pride and self-satisfaction are not qualities in any list of spiritual achievements, and Jesus was far from considering wholesome those who had them. Jesus felt that hope lay only in those who had a real sense of guilt.

In recognizing the normal problem of guilt, and in trying to help men by removing the sense of guilt and by giving them new power to avoid doing and being what they feel is wrong, Christianity did indeed recognize one of the deepest problems of humanity. In its attempt to give men a new moral power Christianity has not succeeded completely, as a glance at the history of Christians in action abundantly shows. And it has helped only individuals; each generation has had to face the problem anew. But the number of Christians through the ages who have felt "the burden of their sins roll away," and who have "become new creatures in Christ Jesus," is beyond all statistics.

Now such a change as this is essentially the purpose of all psychiatry, though psychiatry uses other myths and means. What the modern man tends to forget is that the problem was recognized and a therapy offered by the early Christians. Their therapy was quite as high in its effectiveness as is modern psychotherapy. Comparisons in such matters always tend to be odious, and statistics are utterly lacking. We cannot (as both psychotherapists and traditional Christians tend to do) argue the matter by contrasting the successes of one group with the failures of the other. As a matter of fact the two approaches differ in terms and means more than in substance. Certainly the Christian successes have been possible because of the profound psychological insight of the founders of the faith. For Christianity, like all religions, has been the psychiatry of the ages, and Christianity won out over its early rivals because it offered a psychotherapy so much better than theirs.

Salvation is a term we need not fear at all—it

SALVATION

means radical psychotherapy. Of course, the term has been used to mean acceptance for heaven, but the best religious teachers of all ages have meant more than that. They have meant an elevation above the ordinary human condition which will, true, be rewarded in the next life, but only because the elevation was so genuine in this life. This elevation, the mastering of the problems and impulses which fill us with guilt, can be indifferently called salvation or psychotherapy.

The psychological basis on which the therapy of Christianity has been founded is by no means so familiar that it need not be described.

The ancients used terminologies different from any current today to describe the problems a man feels within himself, but since even modern terminology, such as the Freudian, is suggestive rather than definitive, we need not be confused by the differences.

The Christians were not the first to feel inner tensions and guilt. The mass of people, Jews and pagans, rid themselves of guilt by ritualistic exercises, as the mass of Christians have done ever since. The Jews very simply spoke of an evil impulse and a good impulse operating in every man. This we should today describe as the urge to conform to what we accept in the ego ideal as the good, and the perversity of the id in rebelling against it. The Greeks had several approaches to the problem, but in general they agreed in thinking that in every man there is a divine presence, a sort of higher mind, and when this mind "thinks straight," as they termed it, or properly "perceives," it recognizes the true principles of moral obligation. Over against this is the principle of "desire" (close to the libido of Freud's id) which is in constant revolt against this higher perception. The higher perception of the Greeks became in time the traditional "conscience," which means "knowledge" of the good. Its place was taken for Freud by the ego ideal, less adequately by his superego or censor.

The ancients regarded conscience as a divine presence within man, an organ of metaphysical perception. Modern schools tend to regard it as a summation of conditioned reflexes, or as the subjectivized presence of one's parents. Neither attitude need obscure from us the identity of the two in practical function.

For the ancients saw as well as the moderns that over against our urges, or instincts, to gratify the desires of the senses, or to assert our individualities in antisocial aggressiveness, there stands a highly active center with quite different motivation. It is oriented not in our physical and personal desires, but in our ideals and in the demands of society, and it has power to make us terribly uncomfortable, if not to drive us quite insane, if we disregard it.

Here is the basic paradox beneath almost all other paradoxes in our lives. We are equally driven to conform to society and the ideals society has given us, and to revolt against them in the name of our individual desires, indeed our desire for individual existence. With both these urges we must live all our lives, and effect some sort of balance between them.

Salvation

Is this a problem of psychology, psychiatry, or religion? All I can say is that however much the modern practice of psychiatry is invading the field, it is a brash newcomer, and that until fifty years ago no one would have dreamed that the problem was any other than religious, or would have felt that anything but divine grace would help in the inner warfare between them, and its attendant sense of guilt.

When I begin to talk about the problem and state it in this way to my pupils, they all see at once that I am talking about a religious problem—except those majoring in psychology. These are apt to think that religion has been banished to the peripheries where scientific psychology does not concern itself, while this essential problem of ambivalence and guilt is now their own. It is hard for them to admit that modern psychology has not just newly discovered this ambivalence, or to understand that people have been deeply concerned with it for as long as we know human thought. Yet certainly it was central in the minds of the ancient Egyptians, and is expressed in the earliest extended records of human thinking, the Pyramid Texts of 2500 B.C. Throughout all these ages to the present, and even in the present for all but the few who think in terms of psychiatry, the problem of the inner warfare, with its attendant sense of failure and guilt, has been a religious problem. The "good impulse" always seemed to man to be of divine origin, and the revolt against it by the "bad impulse" has been a revolt against God which only God could forgive or overcome.

Toward a Mature Faith

Since man has been so deeply concerned with the problem for so long a time, it would be strange indeed if his attempts to deal with it had all been completely futile, and that only in the present years have we come into the beginnings of wisdom.

The Christian versions of the struggle and its solution all go back to Paul's account of it. Paul had been a convinced and carefully observant Jew, who had tried in every way to keep the Jewish Law in its strictest form. But he had found that Law a problem. He never, even as a Christian, questioned the rightness of the moral standards set forth in the Jewish Law. In this he was not so radical as Jesus is reported to have been, when he said that the Old Testament provision of an eye for an eye was not morally or legally valid. Paul challenged no text of Scripture.

Furthermore, Paul had no specific problem comparable to that of a modern person who, brought up in a church which condemns divorce, begins to want a divorce and hence to wonder whether after all divorce is always wrong. To Paul there never was the least doubt that what the Law forbade (things which incidentally the better-minded pagans also disapproved) was wrong, and that its positive commands were "holy, righteous, and good." But while he "delighted in the Law after the inner man," and approved and accepted it completely in his conscience, he had found that the Law was actually his chief impetus to break it! For as soon as the Law had said to him "Don't covet," instantly he had begun to covet.

SALVATION

He found, that is, exactly what the Freudians have thought was their new discovery, that "the id knows no negatives." Every prohibition is, for our id, or for our basic individualistic natures, actually a positive suggestion. To give a two-year-old child a box of beans or beads to play with, while telling him not to put them up his nose, is to invite him to put them up his nose. You as his mother or father may have established such controlling influence that he will not do it, but most children will put them up their noses the moment you are not looking.

The wise parent will not anticipate with any but the most urgent prohibitions, since every prohibition, if it does not provoke disobedience, suggests it and does create a moral problem in the child. "Stolen fruits are the sweetest," just because there is such sweetness in breaking the law against stealing. In breaking any law there is sweetness for one part of us, but if we are sensitive, there is bitterness and guilt for the rest of us. Of course, this talk about our "parts" is metaphorical, like all psychological terminology, but we do not know enough to describe our experiences and emotions in direct terms.

All of us but the extreme "healthy minded" will know how Paul felt. He could keep himself from positive acts of adultery, theft, and murder; but coveting? desire? pride? Malicious thoughts that come out in unconscious acts of cruelty? Most of us cannot keep ourselves even from overt "sins of the flesh," that is, acts openly and directly against the code. But even the most strictly observant may, and usually do, feel guilty for the subtler assertions of the id, what Paul called the "old man" in us.

In very large proportion the people who go to the psychiatrist broken down, on the verge of a complete depression, with a "guilt complex," have lived what in general would be considered quite exemplary lives. They find that their sense of guilt arises from little things done, or even contemplated, in childhood. It is not the wicked Catholics but the very best of them who go most often to confession. One might almost say that an abiding sense of unworthiness and guilt is an important part of every "fine" personality. And the experience such a person has is that his "better" nature is condemning his "worse" nature. As Paul described it, he recognized with delight the rightness of what seemed to him God's will for him, but there was a law of his very nature which made him revolt and do the wrong thing. So with the "mind," or conscience, or superego, he served the Law of God: but with the "flesh," or id, he served the law of sin. "Wretched man that I am!" his "I" or ego very naturally exclaimed.

From this basic and timeless experience Paul went on to doctrines where the modern man does not follow him so easily. That human perversity is inherited from the sin of Adam, as Paul carefully explains, will mean nothing to us who think in terms of evolution. The doctrine of predestination we may accept as the inevitability that this division within ourselves is the pattern of human nature, and that we can no more escape from

SALVATION

human nature than a dog from being a dog. Many of us, myself included, revolt from the picture of a God who, as Paul says, made some of us "vessels of honor . . . prepared in advance for glory" while "to show forth his wrath and glory" he made the rest of us "vessels of dishonor . . . prepared for destruction."

This doctrine, while accepted by many Catholics and especially emphasized by Luther and Calvin, was always repellent to the majority opinion in the Catholic churches, as it has largely become to most Protestants. The doctrine was a natural and logical conclusion from the experience that Paul himself had, as we shall see, but logical conclusions are as dangerous in religion as they are in most of life. My only point in mentioning these two mythological (or theological) settings for Paul's sense of guilt is to show that his psychological analysis, his sense of actual motivation, should not be confused with them.

Even the most closely scientific modern thinker usually draws larger implications from his data than they will actually substantiate. A later generation strips those away, as Einstein has done with Newton, and the older scientist at last stands for his actual contribution, not for the larger conclusions. So with Paul. His understanding of the problem of guilt is not to be belittled because he put that understanding in a cosmic context which perhaps we cannot accept, which, indeed, the majority opinion in Christian tradition has never fully accepted.

Yet to every man his due, and much is due to Paul.

He saw the basic fact that mere teaching of right and morality is not enough. We can live lives "without inner condemnation" only as our whole personalities are aligned to what we consider to be right. Merely to be taught what is right may indeed put us among the devils, not the saints, for, as another early Christian said, "The devils also believe, and tremble." Man must somehow, say both Christians and psychiatrists, be brought to accept with the whole man, the entire personality, what our minds or consciences consider right. Otherwise, in Jesus' phrase, the last state will be worse than the first.

The early Christians not only were aware that this is the central problem of living—they were excellent diagnosticians—but they went on to a real therapy. The therapy of the pagan world had been basically of two kinds. The first was the one offered by the Greek philosophic schools whose influence carried on into Roman (and our own) times. It was the belief that by training the mind to contemplate and hence to appropriate, superhuman reality, whether in Platonic, Aristotelian, or Stoic form, the higher mind would be strengthened to the point that it could master the lower desires and impulses. This itself could be done in two ways, first by developing a cold aloofness from society, and from all desires and personal attachments, so that money, luxury, even friends and family, seemed quite unimportant and dispensable because one had developed complete self-sufficiency. Secondly, the training might be to rise to a mystical association with higher

SALVATION

reality. In both solutions the essential emphasis was upon training oneself in a sense of true reality and of values. Plato, the Stoics, and many others wrote beautiful documents in this vein which we still can read with deep profit.

Such an approach, however, is too hard, too rarefied, for the average man today, as it was quite beyond the scope of most people in antiquity. We still get benefit and inspiration for doing the right by having the right movingly presented to us, by thinking in terms of it. But we return to our sense of guilt, which is largely a sense that we are doing what our superego, or ego ideal, condemns.

The ancients had supposed that this inner perception of truth and right was evidence that a bit of the mind of God was within us. Christianity has called it our conscience, and made it into the voice of God speaking to us. Now, it seems to me, we have learned from psychology one clear thing, namely, that this part of us originates in our parents' approval or disapproval. It begins in each of us not with a metaphysical sense of right, but with the standards of conduct which our mothers and fathers represented to us as children. In childhood it was a matter of the personal adjustment of our infantile desires and gratifications to the demands of the adults who controlled us.

As we grew older these experiences, and those persons, became a part of ourselves, so that we now rebuke ourselves as our parents used to rebuke us. The parents became a part of our inner being in the form of our conscience. We still experience that part of ourselves as personalities, as our "better selves," as "the voice of God," that is, in a distinct personal relationship. An adult may project this personal conscience onto his wife, his analyst, his God, his priest, for the great majority of us can deal with it only in personal terms.

Everywhere man has tended to put his gods into human form. Primitive man often represented his gods in animal form, and there are still tribes who prefer this type of representation. Children go through such a stage in their love of animal stories, in their fetishism with stuffed animals, in their passion for pets. This love of animals is a normal part of mature persons, though it is by no means so universal in adults.

But the God of our conscience is not a bear or a dog. It is a person. And the more mature peoples all over the earth represent their gods in human form. Devotions are normally carried out before a picture or image in that form, however crudely it is represented. We call the images of other religions "idols"; if we are old-fashioned Protestants or Jews, we tend to regard even Christian images as idolatrous. But such images have been the universally spontaneous product of human nature and human need—the need to feel that in dealing with the great Power which controls all things and sets the standards of human life and conduct for all men and within ourselves, we are dealing with a person. The concern of Protestant theologians to demonstrate the "personality of God" is only the Protestant version of this same phenomenon.

Salvation

People of the ancient world felt, however, that this person, or these persons, must not only have personality; they must also have had personal experiences analogous to human experiences. In the early stories the gods had such varied adventures that thoughtful Greeks, like Plato, considered the exploits of the gods not fit to be told to children. As men's sense of right developed, the experiences of the gods were much restricted. But some of the notions persisted, though few of the saving gods of antiquity presented all the features together.

One was the conception of a divine family consisting of father, mother, and child. Often one of the parents was a human being. The birth of the child by union of human and divine, as set forth in many myths, was most important, for here was the resolution of the tension between the higher and lower. In their loving union they had produced together a perfect being in which both the higher and the lower were represented, as, it is our experience, they are in ourselves. Similarly, though the child was usually a hero, like Hercules or Harpocrates, he was commonly destroyed by wicked forces, and then restored to life, to immortal life. Divine suffering was everywhere presented as part of the hope of man's salvation.

The psychological implications of these and many other details in ancient dreams of the saving god have by no means been adequately explored. Here we must keep in mind for the moment only the fact that salvation was thought by the ancients to be won by personal relation with a personal deity.

Toward a Mature Faith

A beautiful story of such a salvation was told by Apuleius in his famous book, *The Golden Ass*. Here a man sunk in sin is depicted as bewitched and changed into an ass. He is transformed back into human shape when the goddess Isis appears to him in person and instructs him to eat roses carried by a priest in her procession. From this first step he goes on into superhuman life as he completes the rites of Isis and her divine consort, Osiris. The ancients, however, had found such divine personalities sporadic, hard to reach, and only vaguely personal.

It was Christianity which first triumphantly announced that the true divine person had actually come down to earth in human form, born of God and a human mother; that he had been torn in violent death by evil doers, but had defeated all the forces of evil by rising from the dead and making himself available for men. This was not a remote mythological dream, the early Christians said, but an event of recent history. He had taken upon himself the guilt of the world, and its destructive power had itself been destroyed with his death. With him one could now be identified, and in that identification the old man, the selfish, rebellious instincts in us, would die, and the higher principle in us come into new birth, new existence. "There is therefore now no condemnation to those who are in Christ Jesus," Paul exclaimed. The newly born "mind of the spirit" brings the ego "life and peace."

Paul's language is violent in the extreme. He has "crucified" his flesh with Christ; he has killed its activities; he now beats it down and keeps it in complete enslavement to his better nature. He has still a hard struggle, and he has no sense that he can relax his vigilance. He dreams of a time when his "body" also will be redeemed, but though this has not happened, he is no longer the slave of his lower nature. The terror which was guilt is gone and now he, Paul, is the son of God also, a joint heir with Christ, who can look to God with confidence, and say "Father." While Paul struggles, Christ sits beside God the Father, interceding for him.

In pagan antiquity we can find ideas and suggestions similar to many details of this picture, but nothing before Christianity offered this concreteness and conviction. And nothing has ever brought a solution of the problem of guilt to so many people, or given to so many power actually to live by their ideals rather than by their immediate desires and impulses. Christians have lived by, with, and in, the constant presence of their living personal savior. Belief that a personal God and a divine Christ can help does bring a sense of forgiveness, as well as constructive power to live by our ideals.

This great help of the ages the modern intellectual, and the great mass of imitators of what they think is the intellectual fashion, have abandoned. There have been gains from that rejection, but also cruel losses. The true intellectual, that is, one whose analytical thinking really dominates his life, is as exceptional a person now as he was in antiquity. Such people can return to the solutions of the pagans, and have done so. There is, for example, the relatively small group of people who are turning to the Perennial Philosophy of mysticism (Leibnitz, not Aldous Huxley, invented the term). They are reading the ancient mystics with the mystics of India, China, and Islam, as well as of Judaism and Christianity. But these are now, as they were in antiquity, a group apart.

The mass of intellectuals have turned instead to the ancient solution of self-sufficiency: Nietzsche with his dream of the Superman who needed nothing from his fellows; the ethical schools and groups who suppose that ethics can be taught (really a return to legalism) and notably led by sincere Jewish people who have given over the old legalism for a new one; people who, like Plato, trust that their reasons will find the right for them; people like Freud who think that through psychological research they will find (or have found) all solutions. In these solutions, each in its own way, the saving person consciously or unconsciously becomes the ego, the self. Hope, for people who entertain it in one form or another, is, contrary to Christian teaching, in themselves. That such people are rarely boastfully self-sufficient, like Nietzsche, or, in his own way, like Freud, must not obscure the fact that in building up ourselves as self-saving agents, we are building up our own personalities with powers which have traditionally been ascribed to God and Christ.

Actually, the ground on which such a personality stands, indeed the self-sufficient personality itself, is quite as mythological as the most elaborately creedal

SALVATION

Christ. That we are not, or in only rare cases can be, saving personalities for ourselves is the fact which only faith can hide from us, and it is the latent sense of our inadequacy which now makes insecure so large a proportion of the intellectual classes. An undergraduate at Yale recently protested violently in print against the futility of certain courses in the Department of Religion (not mine, for he had not studied with me). He admitted in private that his real resentment was that, in taking them, he had not been converted to Christianity and made a churchman of one sort or another. The desire for conversion, for being taken over by a creed and a divine Person, is increasingly one of the distinguishing characteristics of the younger generation of intellectuals.

That is, the myth that we can build ourselves up into being our own saviors is now widely challenged. Yet it is frankly one of my own myths, and it can be a highly constructive one. Indeed it seems to me that through his myths and projections and symbols man has always been his own savior.

Democracy as we know it in America, for example, was founded by people who lived by it, and in its name led man into one of the greatest advances in human history. The implicit philosophy of the American state is that right will be found in an appeal not to God or a church, but to the basic common sense of the average man. A myth indeed! Certainly only faith can hold it. I happen to share that faith, but must admit that no proposition could be less demonstrable from a scientific or factual point of view. Still, my contribution as a citizen largely depends upon my believing the myth, believing in America, accepting the decision of the electorate, and working with the social structure as it is given us. That does not mean that I may not criticize the government, or, if people I do not approve are elected to office, that I will not try to have better candidates elected next time. But my personal adjustment to society, like the personal adjustment of an African tribesman through his tribal organization, will be much more constructive if I believe in my society. However much I may wish to reform it or improve it, I must work with it rather than try to destroy it. In our case it means believing that mankind in the mass will produce true guidance, or the best guidance available. It is a belief in ourselves collectively as the savior.

But no one such myth is enough for us. We are, I said in an earlier chapter, essentially polytheists, and the most common successful adjustment is that we have a variety of mythological frames to suit different aspects of our lives. If I believe that in democracy and in science human judgment will bring us into greater truth, and that as far as possible we must develop a sense of ethical discrimination and responsibility for and within ourselves, the fact remains that I do not live my personal life in terms of political or scientific structure, but in terms of ethics and a sense of values in human conduct, a sense of right and wrong, to which the law of the land and the findings of science are largely indifferent.

We need a myth to frame our personal lives quite

as much as we need a socio-political myth for society. In these fields of private morality, as contrasted with public, the form of myth which always has worked best is a personal one. We need faith in an ideal person, not only as one who tells us what we may or may not do, but who, for all his strictness, loves us and forgives us and is willing and able to help us. For the gift of love and the gift of grace and strength are the same thing.

Where is such a person to be found in our modern world of skepticism and critical thought? Can we make one to order, project into him our ideals, until he becomes the embodiment of what we want to be? This is precisely what I suggest we can do. Indeed we can get the strength of the ages, and the comfort of the ages, by calling that person Jesus. In doing so we shall only be doing what men through the ages have done with the figure of Jesus.

8

JESUS IN THE NEW AGE

On nothing is the average intelligent man more ignorant today than on the history of the person of Jesus in our society. The fact is that historians know very little about the historical Jesus, not enough either to "accept" or "reject" him. The result of historical testing of the Gospel records has been that we know with reasonable certainty only the following:

(1) The Christian movement began when a group of people were convinced they had seen a former teacher of theirs, named Jesus, risen from the dead. This vision seems to have begun in Galilee. The story of the empty tomb appears to be later.

(2) Jesus had almost certainly been crucified. The early Christians would never have invented this disgraceful form of death for their risen Lord. Just why he had been crucified is not clear, but there seems no rea-

son to doubt the story that the charge was political rather than criminal. There seems also no reason to doubt that the accusations were brought by the Jews with vested interests in Jerusalem who found him a nuisance. Such a statement is by no means an accusation against the Jews. People with vested interests, in their own way, every day here and in Russia, are crucifying people—people whose opinions seem a nuisance to them, or a threat to their interests.

(3) Jesus seems to have been a son of Mary, and to have had brothers and sisters, and to have come from north Palestine, Galilee.

Before his crucifixion Jesus taught in various parts of Palestine, but what he taught is disputed at every point. He would appear primarily to have taught something about a coming "kingdom of God" or "of heaven," for it was this teaching which was represented as subversive to Pilate, but how much his accusers or, indeed, his followers, distorted Jesus' teaching of the kingdom we do not know, so that among the conflicting reports of his teaching on the kingdom we can choose only arbitrarily. To him are ascribed a great many miracles, many of which, especially those of healing epilepsy and other diseases, are quite credible; but where to draw the line in these matters between the credible and incredible we do not know. Many beautiful teachings are also ascribed to him, a large part of which he may well have originated, though on not one can we put our finger and say that Jesus said it the way we have it recorded.

Toward a Mature Faith

For from the first, and down to the present, the Jesus of history is hopelessly obscured behind what people have wanted to find in Jesus, and have projected into Jesus. This process began with the writers of the Gospels themselves. The Jesus of the Fourth Gospel is very different from the Jesus of the other three Gospels because its author, and his audience, wanted Jesus to represent something quite different from what the authors of the others wanted. Scholars in general feel that the first three Gospels are closer to the historical Jesus than the fourth, and probably that is right. But how much closer? Was their account of Jesus also largely a wish projection? That it was so to some extent is highly probable. For we can see Luke quoting Jesus as saying "Blessed be ye poor: for yours is the kingdom of God. Blessed are ye that hunger now: for ye shall be filled." This Matthew did not bat an eye in reporting "Blessed are the poor in spirit: for theirs is the kingdom of heaven. Blessed are they which do hunger and thirst after righteousness: for they shall be filled." Did Jesus say this in either form; or, if Luke is more trustworthy here, is he so in other places?

It was the illusion of the nineteenth century that the modern critical and rational mind would find a new healing if we could only rediscover the historical Jesus, and so move from faith to knowledge even in the field of religion. Actually the movement ended in complete failure, to the point that many honest historians rejected even the three points of which I say we may be reasonably sure historically, and were convinced there never

Jesus in the New Age

had been a Jesus at all since the account seemed so synthetic. Their doubts have not been shared by the great majority of historians in the field. But reputable scholars no longer write lives of Jesus, because they know they cannot do so.

Actually we see that the vision of the risen Jesus was a crystallizing agent, the beginning of a new fire which swept over the ancient world. This risen Lord—what was he? Into his person were poured all the dreams of Jews, Syrians, Egyptians, Greeks, and Romans. Each group made a Jesus for itself. He was the true lawgiver. He was the Messiah who was quickly to return and overthrow Rome and all secular government to found the kingdom of God on earth. He was the Son of the Great Mother, and they together presented to man the true nature of the Father. Like the pagan savior gods, he was the one torn, and in the life he gave we were to find life so that it was the dead Christ, like the dead Osiris, to whom men began to say their prayers. He was the divine principle dreamed of by philosophers which came from the ultimate One to bring, like light, like rain, God's nature to man.

He even became the great Roman Emperor *par excellence*, who sat upon a cosmic throne as ruler and judge according to the perfect Law of the universe, his own will. He was one whose gifts came in the waters of baptism, and he gave himself to man to eat and drink in the Communion. In his name the philosophy of the Greeks became theology, and for centuries in the West all that was known of Roman law was what had survived in Canon Law. The spirit of monasticism, of flight from the world, a spirit at least as old as Plato's *Symposium* and the Cynics, came to seem the ideal solution to the despairing citizens of collapsing Rome, and so Jesus became the perfect monk, his mother the ideal nun. When the cry to redeem Palestine from the "infidels" threw all Europe into the hysteria of the crusades, Jesus became the leader of all Christian soldiers marching forth to war. With the later discovery of the lower classes and of their rights Jesus became the carpenter, the ideal workman in whose name the distressed and oppressed could oppose their capitalist slave masters. Christianity became the social gospel. At the same time in schools for the upper classes Jesus was the ideal gentleman. For some, like Bruce Barton, he became the ideal promoter and salesman.

I have mentioned only a few of the Christ-myths which have prevailed. But the point is that as Jesus took on all these successive forms (not one of which has ever perished) the emergence of a new form meant a great human achievement, a great new source of power. The mythical figure in each case became a reality as it made men better theologians, monks, crusaders, social reformers, gentlemen, or salesmen.

That is, the emergence of each new vision of the personality of Jesus has meant the coming of grace and peace and power to men. For with the new Jesus each new pattern of life could align itself. He could be their Leader, and in hailing him men could move out into a new freedom from guilt, frustration, and impotence.

Jesus in the New Age

As Jesus became freshly meaningful, men felt their own lives take on meaning and direction.

I am deeply convinced that this is still the best psychotherapy for the mass of men. There will always be the "healthy minded" who can live without salvation, with a sense that they are able to cope with life alone. But not most of us. We must live with a sense of devotion to a great Personality in whom our ideals are incarnate, and who, we feel, responds to our devotion with personal interest and love. Nothing can take the place of such a personality for the mass of men but emptiness and insecurity and a vague sense of guilt in which our lives are meaningless.

A modern substitute for such an ideal person has been the attempt to idealize some living person. That is quite normal to some extent. A loving husband rarely regards the opinion of his wife as just another person's opinion, her censure as just ordinary disapproval. Certainly the opinions, approval, and disapproval of a parent are far more than an ordinary person's judgment to the child. But with maturity the mother's opinion must be less and less authoritative, however much the mother is still respected. It is deeply destructive, however temporarily inspiring, for adults to find their ideals incarnate in a contemporary living human being. A boy who never becomes truly critical of and detached from his mother is never able to live a full life. A girl who idealizes her father too much will probably never be able to marry, or, if she does, she will make a very poor wife. It is a tragedy when a bright young student becomes so captivated with one of his teachers that he spends his life as a follower of that teacher, working on the lines laid out for him, working out the ideas given him, dominated by the principles and methods, the personality, of the older man. "School pieces" are notoriously inferior in the history of art.

Even more the Great Leader of a people can, indeed must, become their destruction. For, quite apart from the inherent wickedness of Hitler and Mussolini, to say nothing of Lenin and Stalin, the greatest harm they did was in demanding, and getting, uncritical following. No actual human being can be our ideal, without our ideal's shrinking in scope and power. This would have been as true of Jesus as of any other person. If we had known all about the actual historical Jesus, and had been able to reconstruct his pattern of life and had really tried to keep ourselves rigidly to that pattern, Western civilization and science could not have developed as they have done. The power in Jesus as the ideal of Western civilization has been precisely his power to change from age to age, and so to embody what in an earlier chapter we called our projections.

For the gadgets and modern medicine, good as they are, are not enough. They cannot touch the problem of anxiety and guilt within our souls, cannot give life meaning. Leisure, ability to travel by sea, air, and land, and freedom from pain, do not in themselves give life meaning, or develop in us what we may as well continue to call spiritual power. From a purely pragmatic point of view it is still true that this comes from our idealism, our dreams of what we ought to be as persons, and from the adjustment of our basically self-centered impulses to those ideals. Our dreams! That is the word to which we must return without a false sense that our dreams are inappropriate in the modern age of reason. Physical security or wealth are very well in their way, but those who have them without dreams, or whose dreams only create warfare in their souls, are among our most wretched contemporaries.

Of all the dreams which can "save" us by giving us new power and freedom from guilt, still incomparably the best is the dream of a perfect human embodiment of our ideals, with the active sense that this person loves us and lifts us rather than condemns us. It is our dreaming, the poetry, the myths, which can bring us this salvation, not our critical approach to life. In saying this I am not at all returning to the sentimentality of a half century ago.

The present age has by no means lost its power to dream. At the very time when we are most productively scientific and critical, the modern mind, in the new poetry, the new painting, the new sculpture, the new music, is tremendously productive in its search for new imaginative forms. The dreams of the fourteen points of Wilson, of the four points of Marshall, of the One World of Willkie, of the rights of all classes of men everywhere to a decent level of existence, of the right of the bright boy from whatever social level to education commensurate with his native ability, these are all dreams, which go far beyond the dreams of any but our own generation.

In our dreaming we have rejected the Jesus of the Victorian Age as our artists have thrown away the art forms of Landseer or the Renaissance, as our musicians have no more use for the musical conventions of even Beethoven and Schubert, as our poets scorn the poetry of Shelley and Tennyson as models for their expression. True these still are the art and music of most of us, just as the mass of people still can sing "Jesus loves me, this I know" in the spirit of a century ago.

But in rejecting the old forms we have not rejected music, or painting, or architecture, or poetry, or beauty. Religious artists must have the same courage as Cézanne or Van Gogh, the courage to create new forms. In this process we need no more abandon Jesus than musicians are abandoning the piano and violin. For whatever Jesus was originally, ever since the first vision of his resurrection he has been nothing but the instrument through which, and in which, our dreams have taken form. We can no more return to accepting the Victorian Jesus of Hoffman and Moody than to writing poetry à la Shelley, or to painting pictures like Landseer.

Modern historical and psychological study have made it very difficult for us to take the next step. Christians through the ages have projected their types of Jesus without the least awareness that they were projecting, and could call their Jesus the historical Jesus without reserve. They could worship this Jesus without restraint, have all the consolations of his love, with no sense that they were worshipping an image of their own making, and with every scorn for idolaters of other religions.

Let us be factual. The vast majority of the human race has taken its comfort in mirages of their own making. Jews, and their descendants in Christianity and Islam, have taken the amazingly constructive step of abandoning images made with hands for an image made in our hearts. With a great sense of pride in our spiritual superiority, all three of these groups have turned the word "idols" and "idolatry" into a word of reproach. But we do not know God, and anything we worship is bound to be an image of our own making. It has always been so, whether we make it in our hearts (as all people have done) along with the graven images, or find the images in our hearts sufficient.

Now, with the new historical sense and psychological awareness, the fact is apparent for the first time that our objects of worship have always been, must also be, images of our own making. Is this discovery going to crush us, to the point that we can no longer have the inspiration of ideals in a concrete, personal form? The new learning will indeed have impoverished us if that is so.

Still, as my physicist friend says, we cannot go back. Certainly we cannot endure living as mourners in the graveyard where our ideal persons are buried. There is nothing to do but to pick ourselves up and go forward.

One thing is certain, we cannot leave ourselves behind with the dead, or we die with them. We shall go forward, if at all, still as human beings, with the same structure as ever, the same basic needs. All that we will have added is a little knowledge (oh, so little) of how we have been functioning all along.

We must not on that account cease to function! If we must function self-consciously, then let us have the courage to be self-conscious. This is one of the highest and rarest forms of courage, but the modern intelligentsia can save itself, or be saved, only by having that courage.

From here on we are in the world of experiment. Nothing has been tried and found sure. I can no more give a rule for the new form of projection, the newly created Jesus, which will satisfy all sorts and temperaments, than anyone could give a universal formula for the new painting, music, or poetry. We must find the way by experimenting, each for ourselves. All I can do is to offer a few suggestions from my own personal experience.

One way in which we can recover a Jesus who will be a saving power for us is by the old method of proof texts and allegory. That is, we read the old material, the religious classics, but especially the New Testament, and select out of this literature the phrases, the parables, which especially appeal to us. With no regard to contradictions or context, we take these as the essential meaning of Jesus and traditional religion. He will indeed be a son of Belial who can read that literature without being struck over and over with the poignancy and depth, the contemporary value, of many things he finds there. You can do the same with Plato, Epictetus, or Shakespeare, but the value of finding these statements in the New Testament is that they gather together to create our ideal person. They anchor us, as we have every right to be anchored, in the idealism of the past, and in doing so, I have explained, give us hope.

It may seem strange, after all I have said about my experience with the historical method, that I should recommend this way of reading the New Testament. But so far as Jesus is concerned, the Gospels do not need to be read in the historical way by the mass of us, or by any of us in our spiritual quest. We shall admit that this is wish projection on occasion. Generally we shall just beautifully project.

I was much comforted in this blatant inconsistency by a talk given by my friend Samuel Thorne, who is an expert in the history of English law. He pointed out that the history of law must be kept sharply distinct from the practice of law. The historian of law, he explained, reconstructs the setting and origin and purpose of a law from the past, and so tells us its original meaning. But he described how a group of fifty of the leading lawyers of England had agreed that to do this in the courts would vitiate the whole legal structure of society. For slowly, but surely, the law must adjust itself to the changing forms and standards of society, while it keeps its predictability, and guards the stability of society even while society changes and it changes with society.

The courts must never seem to invent new law, but by clever quoting and reapplying of decisions in earlier cases, it must solve the problems of the present. Over and again this comes to be what in religion is called the proof-text method: the finding of some statement in the body of accepted truth which will warrant a basically new point of view.

The stability of English history and society, as contrasted with the history of the nations on the Continent, is a result of the fact that the new has thus grown more freely as the British have reinterpreted parts of the old and disregarded what of the old no longer was applicable. The people on the Continent, on the contrary, took Roman law *en bloc*, upon which they have superimposed constitutions which had to be overthrown by revolutions when they no longer were suitable for new conditions. The continuity of American history has been due to our Constitution's being essentially in the English tradition, especially the Bill of Rights which was quickly added to it, and due also to our use of English common law with its possibility of indefinite "reinterpretation."

The continuity of Jewish history, oddly enough, has had a similar basis. The rabbis who created the

Talmud kept rigorously to the texts of the Bible, which like Philo they often interpreted in terms of Roman law. The process produced their magnificent statement: "The law of the land is Law." That is, every Jew must, in the name of his own legal sanctions, obey the law of the country in which he lives. Even the most advanced Reformed Jews can still feel their secure continuity as Jews while they discard as obsolete a large part of the requirements of their ancestors, because they keep the parts of their tradition which seem still valid, however radically reinterpreted. To do so they go back to the Great Charter of Judaism, the Bible, where they study and quote not so much the Law as the Prophets, though they are glad to use what texts from the legal writings they can.

The invasion of historical attitudes and techniques into the field of religion, especially of Protestantism, has been the main cause of the modern feeling of instability and insecurity, because it has made us lose our sense of right through continuity with traditional standards. It has made us all feel adrift in religious, moral, and personal problems.

In the nineteenth and early twentieth centuries the process of adaptation by reinterpretation was still going on. Only the intellectuals, and relatively few of them, felt the threat of the new history. Tennyson was deeply affected by it, but by fresh interpretation of Christian tradition he could come through to the final stability of his "In Memoriam" in spite of it. Even such an account of Jesus as that of Renan, destructive as it seemed to those who held the old traditions in the old way, went quite beyond historical analysis to construct a positive picture of Jesus, one which by use of selected passages gave an account of him that greatly helped many people for decades. For here was a Jesus who could be theirs, and as the break with the religious past was healed they were given stability and security.

Professor Cadbury of Harvard as an historian has presented us with the modern dilemma most tersely. In his much used little book, *The Peril of Modernizing Jesus*, he showed that the Jesus of history was a man of a long-lost age, and that that Jesus could be understood at all only in terms of his age. The problems with which he was concerned were the problems of a Jew in Palestine under the Roman Empire, and the solutions he offered were solutions of those problems, not ours. In a memorable address to a national group of biblical scholars Cadbury spoke of "The Peril of Archaizing Ourselves," that is of trying to fool ourselves with a sense that our problems can be resolved in the old solutions, language, and formulas. We can neither bring the historical Jesus into our own day, nor return to his. From the historian's point of view Cadbury's position is in my mind unassailable.

Cadbury is an excellent example of a man who has found stability through reinterpretation and application of traditional principles. It would be an impertinence to analyze his private life, but he is publicly famous for his unqualified Quaker loyalties, his opposition to armed force as a solution of any problems, his participation in all sorts of conciliation, his work for the distressed among our former enemies, and his active interest in all sorts of unheralded relief of those who suffer from the various conflicts and rapacities of modern society. That he does this without a strong sense of continuity with Christian tradition I do not for a moment believe. How he has reached this balance even I, who am his personal friend and great admirer both as a scholar and man, do not know. I cite him only as an example of the fact that we need not betray the best of the new to keep the best of the old. But I strongly suspect that rigorous as he is as an historian, for his personal life he is an allegorizer of favorite biblical passages.

Thus far I have said that while we must reinterpret as lawyers do, we cannot modernize the historical Jesus, construct an ideal Jesus for ourselves, and then assert that that was the true Jesus of history. We cannot try to be twentieth-century Renans (though a twentieth-century Renan would get thousands of readers), and yet we do need a Jesus-figure for the twentieth century. What we must do is to use the best of the new to discover the best in the old, and, finding it in our own way, learn to express it in our own way.

From our point of view, what was the best of the old? It was not, as the New-Orthodox try to tell us, in the belittling of man and of human hopes and efforts. It lay, rather, in its expansion of human horizons, its deepening of human faith and hope, its giving man confidence in the constructive aspects of human life. This was supremely expressed in the old doctrine of Incarnation, which meant that the ideal woman could, and did, conceive and bear the divine child.

By implication Jesus taught that this was not a unique event. For he described the Last Judgment, when many who had lived up to all that they had been taught in formal religion would be rejected, while many who had never heard of him, or his lessons, would be welcomed as his friends, his proper associates in heaven. The divine child himself recognized that these too had potential, indeed actual, divine nature, for they had been sensitive to the needs of others, even to so simple a matter as giving a cup of water to a thirsty man. Such divinity was pre-eminently represented in Jesus himself, according to his followers, but he taught that it was manifest also in many people about him. It appeared not only among Jews, but among the despised Samaritans, particularly in a Samaritan whose sympathies extended to a Jew in trouble.

That is, Jesus came to be the incarnation, and so the source for others, of the stability of faith, of the promise of hope, of the creative potency of love. In being the source of these in others he was their salvation. He has always been the great symbol, at once a public one for a church, and a private one for the individual. To the individual he has always, when he brought salvation, taken on the aspects which the individual needed. You may protest that he, as savior, is a myth, not historically and scientifically verifiable as cause and effect. Of course he is a myth. But are we afraid of such a word any more? The sequence, true, is not demonstrable. Yet it has worked, as myth, through the ages to the comfort, stability, and inspiration of men. The contrast between Nietzsche's "Human all too Human" and this saving vision of Jesus, is the contrast between the human limitations that frighten us, and divinity. In the salvation offered by this vision we too become in a measure divine.

So all this little book has had to say is: let us be the age prophesied long ago, when our young men will see visions, and our old men dream dreams. For only through dreams has man ever been saved. Salvation will come to us as we too once again can see visions.

9

PERSONAL AGAIN

The way of life I have been describing is a way of courage and profound faith. It took much faith in our judgments when we gave up the old faiths. Now we know we shall never understand the universe; and we have hope only as we take one step farther, and have faith in our dreams. My own discovery, not original with me, but still my own, was that man has never at any time had faith in anything but his dreams, or in the dreams of his ancestors which he learned in a church. Dreams gave men the great positive assertions by which they have guided and inspired themselves in the past. As we are men we cannot do without these affirmations of meaning and value, and we are still men in that all but the philosophers and mystics among us (who can take care of themselves) need such affirmations embodied in ideal personal form.

Personal Again

The great achievement of a successful psychoanalysis is that the patient, having discovered what manner of man he is, is willing to be that man without all the indirections of his old neuroses. The value of knowing ourselves is that only so can we be ourselves. We must accept ourselves, not in our wickedness and sin, but in our human drive to envisage the perfect, or just the better, and to try to be more and more like it.

As individuals we are walking the plank. For some, the plank is long; for some it is short. We all fall off sooner or later. We do our little bit in the succession of humanity, and then humanity has no more use for us, and nature can no longer sustain us. In such an existence it is very easy to be pessimistic; indeed the pessimist is getting happiness in a masochistic, neurotic fashion. But we all get discouraged and frightened at times, and need the consolation men used to get in prayer.

Can we still pray? What I have to say at the end is that, after all the ground I have covered, I still pray devoutly, and have the consolation of the old "Presence" with which I lived in my youth. And why should I not pray? If men have always addressed their prayers to projections of their highest ideals, as I am convinced is true, still men have been inspired and strengthened as in prayer their ideals became vivid to them. There is no reason in the world why I should not do the same.

To whom, to what, and by what name, shall we pray? It seems obvious to me that we can use the old symbolic name of God or Jesus in our prayers if we are

Toward a Mature Faith

Christians, of the God of our fathers if we are Jews. I see no reason why the fact that we now know that those words have all along been symbols should rob us of them. We cannot make new symbols to order, and there is no reason in the world why we should try to do so. "Jesus," we saw, has been a term, a personalization, into which men have packed the best they knew. We can do the same, and in doing so will find another value in that the name will be our link with the idealism of our fathers, our root in the past. What we need even in our maturity is a firm link with, indeed foundation in, our childhood. It was as children that we learned our most important symbols, and in our most stirring experiences we still turn to them, as it is famous that French anticlericals often use the Church for baptism, marriage, and funerals. In times of deepest meaning we find that only the symbols of childhood can express that meaning. We all can pray.

So I forget my qualifications and quibbles and call upon Jesus—and he comes to me. This is not dishonesty but basic common sense. Man has prayed through the ages because he was so made that he got added strength, sweetness, calm, by thus calling his ideals to him in personal form, and communing with them. *Homo sum.* I too will accept myself as a human being, act humanly, and pray.

What do we pray "for"? Never do we pray "give me" in any way. That prayer we have indeed left behind. Success, safety, even life for ourselves and our loved ones, for these we cannot pray to the sort of God or Jesus I am suggesting. It has been a travesty when men have prayed to an omnipotent God for health, victory, or escape. Even when I still believed in such a God with all my heart I early stopped asking God to change his plans at my convenience. The only true word of prayer, and that quite sufficient, is "make me." Make me big enough to take what comes, loving and just with my fellows, strong to keep on what seems to me the path of right. More like thee, my God, more like thee. For God is the ideal we know we should be. The "imitation of God" is a phrase old in Judaism.

The amazing thing is that as we pray to such a God, calling him God, Jesus, Christ, Mary, whatever we were brought up to say, the Person does come to us, touches us, quiets us, and makes us whole again.

In this experience you, reader, will come with me round the circle. If you still believe, as I do, that the Person to whom you pray is the embodiment of your own ideals, you will come to understand in your heart what I have been saying, that to our formulation there probably corresponds some reality which, like nature itself, is always unknown but still exists. This, however, will seem relatively unimportant since we cannot get beyond our projections. Comparatively few physicists are interested in the nature of reality as it is apart from their formulations. The great thing for the physicist is to get such approximations of reality that he can use them. So the great thing in religion is not to understand the nature of objective spiritual reality, but to find it and use it. For so long as men are men, spiritual reality will always remain the most important factor in human life.

As Uncle Charlie used to say: "Drink deep! Drink deep!"

CPSIA information can be obtained
at www.ICGtesting.com
Printed in the USA
BVHW041138230421
605725BV00013B/186